Praise for *What Great Brands Do*

"If, like me, you've never been a 'brand person,' let Denise Lee Yohn be your guide in building your brand into your business. Follow her principles, embrace her tools, and execute through every single thing you do. As she taught me, that's what great brands do."

  —**B. Joseph Pine II**, coauthor, *The Experience Economy* and *Authenticity*

"While brands have become increasingly complex and challenging to manage, Denise has done a terrific job of breaking down what matters in building brands that don't just thrive, but win."

  —**Scott Davis**, chief growth officer, Prophet, and author, *Building the Brand-Driven Business*

WHAT GREAT BRANDS DO

The Seven Brand-Building Principles

That Separate the Best From the Rest

Denise Lee Yohn

JB JOSSEY-BASS™

A Wiley Brand

Published by Jossey-Bass
A Wiley Brand
One Montgomery Street, Suite 1200, San Francisco, CA 94104-4594—www.josseybass.com

Jossey-Bass books and products are available through most bookstores. To contact
Jossey-Bass directly call our Customer Care Department within the U.S. at 800-956-
7739, outside the U.S. at 317-572-3986, or fax 317-572-4002.

Wiley publishes in a variety of print and electronic formats and by print-on-demand.
Some material included with standard print versions of this book may not be included in
e-books or in print-on-demand. If this book refers to media such as a CD or DVD that is
not included in the version you purchased, you may download this material at http://book-
support.wiley.com. For more information about Wiley products, visit www.wiley.com.

Library of Congress Cataloging-in-Publication Data

Yohn, Denise Lee, 1967-
    What great brands do : the seven brand-building principles that separate the best
from the rest / Denise Lee Yohn.
      pages cm
    Includes bibliographical references and index.
    ISBN 978-1-118-61125-8 (cloth); ISBN 9781118824405 (ePDF);
    ISBN 9781118824337 (ePub)
      1. Branding (Marketing)   2. Brand name products. I. Title.
HF5415.1255.Y64 2014
658.8'27—dc23

                                         2013032239

Printed in the United States of America
FIRST EDITION
HB Printing   10 9 8 7 6 5 4 3 2 1

For Chris

Contents

WHAT GREAT BRANDS DO

Introduction

The most important lesson of history, it's been said, is that people don't learn very much from history.[1] That thought has occurred to me at times when I've heard the offhand comment that Kodak, one of the greatest brands on Earth not that long ago, was ruined by the digital camera. Anyone who believes that a great brand can be undone by mere changes in technology doesn't fully understand what makes great brands great.

Kodak ranked as one of the four most valuable brands in the world in 1996, just behind Disney, Coca-Cola, and McDonald's.[2] It had earned that ranking after decades of being the dominant U.S. maker of affordable cameras and photographic film. Kodak was known as "America's storyteller," and its advertising delivered powerfully memorable messages such as "Kodak, for the times of your life." The "Kodak moment" even became a pop-culture catchphrase. Kodak's name was seared into the public's consciousness as being synonymous with good times and fond memories.

When Kodak filed for bankruptcy in 2012, it had lost $30 billion in market value in the fourteen short years since its profits peaked in 1999.[3] The cause of Kodak's stunning fall has been

1

attributed to claims that Kodak was too slow to move to digital photography, and that it failed to make quality digital-age products. Poor strategic planning, lack of foresight, and inept product development and design have all been claimed as contributing factors.

There is no question that digital photography eroded Kodak's high-profit film and developing businesses. But what if Kodak's many inadequate responses to this challenge were mere symptoms of a deeper problem at Kodak? What if all of the company's disappointments and failures during its years of decline were really rooted in one central failure—a failure to follow through on an integral brand strategy? What if Kodak failed simply because Kodak no longer did what great brands do?

This book is an examination of how great brands manage to avoid the fate of Kodak and other faded companies by using their brands as management tools to fuel, align, and guide every person in the organization and every task they undertake. I show how companies as diverse as IBM, REI, Starbucks, and IKEA have all successfully relied on a management approach that drives their culture, company operations, and customer experiences—an approach I call "brand as business." With brand as business, the brand is the central organizing and operating idea of the business. Great brands use the brand-as-business management approach to grow and succeed in tough economic climates, regardless of the size of their marketing budgets. The seven guiding principles of *What Great Brands Do* and their accompanying action steps and exercises provide a step-by-step methodology for putting your company's brand where it belongs—in the driver's seat of your organization.

Beyond Advertising: Brand as Business

As companies with great brands demonstrate, brand building is in no way confined to advertising and marketing. The proliferation of social networks and the pervasiveness of marketing in recent years may give the impression that companies should elevate the brand communication function, but growth in brand equity and influence comes from an entirely different way of thinking about and using brands. Brand building involves *operationalizing* the brand as an integral way of managing and growing a business. So this book is for business leaders, owners, and general managers—the people who drive the culture, core operations, and customer experiences of an organization. These are the people who can ensure their companies unleash the full potential of their brands.

The trouble is that most companies don't view their brand this way at all. Most leaders don't realize that they need to operationalize their brand. That's because brands are often misunderstood or misrepresented. The idea of brand is more often perceived as a tool for appealing to external audiences—in marketing, PR, maybe even sales. I've heard people define a brand as a company's name, logo, image, advertising, aura, personality, look and feel, attitude, reputation, or trademark.

But the fact is, none of these are your brand. These are manifestations, symbols, or expressions of your brand—and by limiting the definition of your brand to this external, surface level, you fail to realize its full business value. As you examine the principles that drive the world's greatest brands, you will see the correct, complete view: a brand is a bundle of values and attributes that define the value you deliver to people through the entire customer experience, and the unique way of doing business that forms the basis of your company's relationships with all of its stakeholders. Simply put, your brand is *what* your company does and *how* you do it. Your brand is not what you say you are—it's what you do.

This book profiles brands that *do* extraordinary things. Whether large enterprises or small businesses, corporations or nonprofits, business-to-business (B2B) or business-to-consumer (B2C) operations, brand new or a century old, these organizations have operationalized, not simply expressed or marketed, their brands. And by doing so, they have built great ones.

Qualifying Great Brands

What does it take to qualify as a great brand? Profitability is the obvious primary criterion. Great brands tend to have above-average profit margins within their respective categories. Research by strategy consulting firm Vivaldi Partners shows that consumers are willing to pay more for a great brand's products than for competitors' products.[4] Young & Rubicam's Brand Asset Valuator also shows a higher *energized differentiation*, the term the firm uses to characterize a brand's vision, invention, and dynamism, for great brands when compared to their competitors, as well.[5] Then there are the industry lists. Great brands are usually found at or near the top of Interbrand's Best Global Brands Report, the Stengel 50 list of the world's fastest-growing brands, and the Fortune magazine 100 Best Companies to Work For.[6] The brands I chose to include in this book met one or more of these criteria. Many met most of them.

Beneath the measures of profitability and industry esteem that serve as evidence of these brands' greatness, though, is a crucial common underpinning that distinguishes them: companies with great brands conceive of their brands as complete strategic platforms. They identify the key values and attributes that define their brands and then make their brands their businesses—that's what I mean by "brand as business." Operationalizing the brand in this way produces results by optimizing the very core operating system of the business. Brand building of this kind, when it's done well, permeates the company culture, improves the value delivered to customers, and determines how the company interacts with all its stakeholders.

Research shows that only a small portion of companies practice brand building with this brand-as-business approach.

A survey of chief marketing officers and brand managers by the Association of National Advertisers showed that 64 percent say their brands do not influence decisions made at their companies.[7] Brands may drive communications activities, but little else. This means that nearly two-thirds of companies are pouring millions of dollars into marketing and advertising without aligning their business strategies with the values and attributes they're communicating! In each of these companies, brand building remains a costly, discrete, and subjective set of activities. As a result, the full business value of the brand itself goes unrealized.

The Gap Between Advertising and Business

Gap, Inc. provides a case of how a company can falter when high-profile advertising campaigns fail to deliver any real brand-driven value to its customers. In the 1990s, the company's flagship brand, Gap, was considered the darling of the retail apparel industry. The brand practically defined hip, with its popular advertising campaigns and trend-right products. But beginning in 1999, Gap started to lose its luster. It fell out of touch with the new generation of consumers flocking to the malls, and it lagged behind the retail industry's typical five-to-seven-year remodel cycle for its stores.

The company responded by turning to what had seemed to be its most powerful weapon—advertising. Over the next few years, the company launched several big-budget ad campaigns, including a media spend of $130.6 million during 2006.[8] The lavish campaign for the product (RED) collection—with its Annie Leibovitz photographs of Bono, Penelope Cruz, and other celebrities—consumed $58 million alone.[9]

After all that spending, Gap's comparable store sales—retailing's key metric—were down 7 percent for the year.[10] In the estimation of Gene Pressman, former CEO of upscale clothing retailer Barney's, Gap's product offerings at the time failed to live up to the hype. "What's the point of having a really cool story to tell if you don't have anything to sell?" he writes in *Chasing Cool: Standing Out in Today's Cluttered Marketplace*. "Marketing might get people through the door, but they'll walk out the door when there's nothing to buy."[11]

Microsoft made a similar strategic blunder in 2008 when it responded to Apple's snarky "I'm a Mac" advertising campaign with a $300 million advertising counterattack, kicked off with a spot featuring comedian Jerry Seinfeld and Microsoft's iconic founder Bill Gates.[12] The market research firm Brand Keys surveyed Apple and Microsoft users before and after the Microsoft advertising campaign, and discovered that the campaign left both groups with more negative perceptions of Microsoft in the areas of innovation, technology, trouble-free design and warranty, and pricing.[13]

Unreliable outcomes from advertising may be more widespread than most people are aware. J. C. Larreche, professor of marketing at INSEAD, found that more marketing spend is not a key determinant for company growth. In fact, in the period between 1985 and 2004, Fortune 1000 firms that decreased their marketing spend actually delivered the highest growth in market capitalization— growth that outstripped the Dow Jones by 80 percent.[14]

Great brands such as Google, Lululemon Athletica, and the Body Shop have made this case in their own ways, managing to grow enormously with little advertising. The clothing retailer Zara, in stark contrast with Gap, has done minimal advertising outside new-store announcements and twice-yearly sales promotions. And yet Zara grew to over 1,600 stores and $9.2 billion in sales with marketing expenditures averaging just 0.3 percent of revenue, compared with the typical 3 percent to 4 percent among its competitors.[15]

I don't mean to suggest that companies don't need to advertise. Advertising isn't good or bad per se, but advertising that is divorced from the realities of the company's actual offering can be counterproductive, as the research on the Microsoft campaign showed. The picture for Gap has actually brightened in recent years as noticeable improvements in product design and shopping experience have been supported and expressed through its successful "1969" marketing campaign.

Operationalizing Instead of Advertising

When viewed through the lens of the brand-as-business approach, it becomes clearer why Kodak failed even though, contrary to popular belief, Kodak's management didn't lack for innovation or foresight. In fact, it was a Kodak engineer in 1975 who invented a toaster-sized contraption that was the world's first digital camera.[16] Just six years later, in 1981, an internal research document predicted that digital imaging would inevitably do great damage to Kodak's film business, and that the company had approximately ten years to manage the transition.[17] Management responded by investing $5 billion in digital image research and filing more than a thousand digital imaging patents.[18] Kodak was neither unprepared for nor incapable of meeting the digital challenge. Kodak's years of poor management, poor strategy, and poor execution were all symptoms of a more fundamental problem at the company.

What went wrong? From the brand-as-business standpoint, Kodak failed to continue to operationalize its brand. The company put its short-term business imperatives in the driver's seat and neglected to adapt its brand values and attributes to the opportunities of the new digital age:

- Kodak's culture during the transition to digital extolled a commitment to engineering excellence and to the company's technological "core competencies," instead of reaffirming the brand's reason for being and the company's expertise in helping customers enjoy unique emotional experiences.

- Kodak pitched new products to the public instead of connecting emotionally with people in new ways *through* those products.
- It followed trends started by others (introducing its Easyshare camera well after the field was filled with options from Canon and others, for example), chased after fickle consumers (attempting to reach the younger generation of Internet pioneers when Baby Boomers who had grown up with Kodak remained a viable market with a range of needs for digital images), and allowed consumer behaviors to direct the company's efforts instead of using its brand essence to drive innovation and anticipate what people would really want.
- It lacked the attention to detail in its discrete offerings (initially releasing photo printers with poor quality and slow output speed, for example); moreover, it missed the opportunity to present a seamless end-to-end digital imaging experience.
- It failed to create shared value throughout the ecosystem of product developers, service providers, software developers, social media channels, and influential customers that comprised the new digital world.

As it turns out, all these Kodak missteps are the precise opposite of what great brands do. Consumers gravitated toward competitors who executed better than Kodak, as the company lurched from one strategy to the next, leaving others to fill the void left by a once-great brand that lost its way.

Setting Your Brand GPS

I single out Kodak not because its story is so unusual but because it is the grandest and most recent example of a widespread problem in corporate leadership. Breaking from your brand, ignoring your culture, following trends, chasing consumers, and running roughshod over details are all very common errors. Some of the best and brightest executives make these mistakes all the time despite the best of intentions. And these mistakes happen at even the best of companies.

I know this firsthand because I worked at Sony Corporation's electronics division during the height of the industry's transition to digital technology. My colleagues and I saw the advantages that the Sony brand had enjoyed for so many years start to slip away, as fast followers ripped off our designs, features, and technology and then sold copycat products at a fraction of our price. We saw other pioneers navigate the emerging convergence of hardware, software, and services more quickly and skillfully than we did. We understood that we could no longer take our brand strength for granted and that we needed new ways to leverage our brand value.

But despite the warning signs that began to go off back then, we struggled to think differently and make changes. I personally experienced the difficulties of challenging ingrained ways of doing things that have produced success in the past. So I understand the hurdles you will face in attempting to replace any tried-and-true practice by applying the principles in this book. Nonetheless, these principles have been proven out by the experiences of some of the best companies in the world. In writing this book, I've often thought that this is precisely the kind of guide that my colleagues and I at Sony really needed years ago to help us find our way.

In that light, I return to Kodak to offer this final cautionary note: during the years when the seeds of Kodak's demise were sown, the company was highly profitable and successful. When Kodak's profits peaked in 1999, it was well after the revolution in digital cameras had begun. Kodak executives at the time no doubt believed that they were managing the company's transition to digital and away from film well. They continued to invest billions in research and product development, assuming those massive investments would pay off. With each successive CEO, Kodak executives kept thinking that the next strategy, the next product, would restore the Kodak brand name to its former glory. They probably thought that right up until it was too late.

Perhaps your company, like most companies, is succeeding today without a brand-as-business approach. In that case, you might want to consider what you're leaving on the table by not fully operationalizing your brand today. Your company may be doing well, but is it really thriving? And are your current activities on behalf of your brand helping lay the foundation for continued growth? Or is it possible that your brand right now is coasting, thanks to some favorable winds at its back?

And as you read on, you should ask yourself, what about tomorrow? If your brand is not being used as your company's figurative GPS today, if it's not driving what the company does and how it does it, what will determine the company's direction when the market changes without warning, as markets always do? What happens when a crisis comes, since every business faces a crisis sooner or later? Have you built a great brand that can withstand the threat of such negative forces? Will your company have the clarity of a brand vision to remake itself, as IBM and other great brands have? Or will it be more apt to go the way of Kodak?

The Seven Brand-Building Principles That Power Great Brands

The book outlines how companies don't just use their brands as symbols or messages to gain a competitive edge but as strategic management tools to change the game completely. It is organized into chapters that correspond with what I see as the seven most distinctive, defining characteristics or principles of what great brands do. In some cases the principles describe what great brands *don't* do, because oftentimes the most important decisions a company can make are choices about what not to do.

Each chapter presents exercises, tools, and action steps that I recommend you undertake, based on my twenty-five years of consulting work with dozens of Fortune 1000 brands. These principles and exercises are not meant as a substitute for the thorough brand audit and reappraisal required to reorient a company toward a brand-as-business approach. My hope instead is that thinking over these principles and doing the exercises—and discussing them with your peers—will help you elevate the current conversation about brand building. The traditional definition of the brand as a mere marketing asset needs to end—the sooner the better. This book represents my modest contribution toward the old definition's speedy demise.

I start with Principle One, "Great Brands Start Inside." Cultivating a corporate culture in brand building is of primary importance. Culture change is the necessary first step in any effort to define or redefine the company's brand, because culture determines whether the brand is embraced and appropriately interpreted and reinforced by all the brand's many stakeholders, including vendors, distributors, agencies, and strategic partners. For instance, if suppliers are not on board with the values and attributes that define your brand, delivery of brand value is likely to be compromised by shoddy manufacturing or shipment delays. When a brand-as-business approach begins with culture, each strategic initiative reinforces the cultural values and attributes that define the brand. IBM is an impressive case of remaking a brand by remaking corporate culture, but there are many others.

The second principle, "Great Brands Avoid Selling Products," is about the importance of developing superior emotional connections though products, rather than relying on product superiority alone. The best products do not always win out, for the simple reason that people don't rationally assess a product's features when making a purchase decision. People buy according to how brands make them feel, or what identity they help them experience and express. The chapter shows how Nike's iconic "Just Do It" campaign wouldn't have happened if company executives hadn't rejected a proposed campaign that failed to meet this standard. The methods included demonstrate how you can reach beyond your brand's current category and make emotional connections through unmet needs and hidden consumer demand.

"Great Brands Ignore Trends" is the third principle of what great brands do. Trends may help attract attention in the short term, but they can change so quickly that you always put your brand identity at risk by following them. As Starbucks, Chipotle, and others have shown, it is far more important to anticipate and interpret larger cultural movements if your brand is to have enduring resonance. Completing the Brand Diagnostic exercise in this chapter will help you see where your company may be missing out on opportunities to decipher and interpret changes on the horizon and sustain your brand relevance and cultural resonance over time.

The fourth principle, a corollary to the third, is "Great Brands Don't Chase Customers." Chasing customers holds the same temptation as following trends, and it exacts a similar toll—compromising brand identity for the sake of increased short-term revenue. Great brands ranging from Red Bull to Lululemon succeed by maintaining their brand integrity and accepting that the brand is not for everyone. If you identify your best target customers and focus on the unique value you bring them, you strengthen your brand as well as your ties to these customers.

Principle Five, "Great Brands Sweat the Small Stuff," recognizes the elevated expectations that consumers now place on brands. Organizational silos almost guarantee gaps in the customer experience of your brand. Great brands, with REI as one example, go to great lengths to close these gaps—and they do it as integral expressions of their brands. Action steps for this principle include creating a Customer Experience Architecture to identify optimal experiences for consumers in each of your channels, and using a Brand Touchpoint Wheel to assess, align, and strengthen the impact of your brand.

Principle Six, "Great Brands Commit and Stay Committed," is one of the most difficult principles to uphold, and one that only the greatest brands do well. From Shake Shack to Vanguard, this chapter focuses on the opportunities these great brands consciously and deliberately forgo out of their long-term commitment to their brand identities. They will sacrifice the sacred—short-term profit and growth—to maintain brand integrity. This chapter discusses ways to clarify the essence of your brand and build a brand platform that establishes the competitive advantages you never want to compromise.

The final principle, number seven, is "Great Brands Never Have to 'Give Back.'" Great brands make their social and cultural contributions by creating shared value for all stakeholders, including their communities. If through the first six principles you are able to construct an enduring vision of your brand, you are then set to resolve your brand's social and cultural relevance. Consumers are tiring of companies that take with one hand and "give back" with the other. Great brands manage to use the power of their brands to inspire change and have an overall beneficial impact on society. IKEA's brand mission to improve people's lives, for instance, is more than a marketing strategy—it's a true brand-as-business effort to provide widespread accessibility of its products by designing and operating the company with low prices at its core.

The presentation of these seven principles in their own chapters does not imply that they are efforts to be adopted independently. In Chapter Eight, I explain that great brands practice all seven principles because no individual principle holds enough power to transform a business. In fact, brand as business is an integrated approach that requires commitment to and vigilant execution on all of the principles. It may seem logical to start by focusing on one or two principles and ignoring both the ones you think you've dealt with and the ones that look hard to implement. But chances are, the latter types of principles are going to be the ones that will do your brand the most good. This final chapter discusses how each principle relates to and supports the others, and explains the need for brand as business to be embraced as an enterprise-wide approach.

The book ends with a call for ownership of the brand-as-business approach at the highest level of any organization. In my experience, what separates a truly great brand from one that is merely good is whether the company is capable of a complete and thorough implementation of its brand as its business. Only when leaders of your company galvanize the organization to adopt these seven principles can yours be transformed into a great brand.

Invest in Brand Building

Try for a moment to imagine your brand as a source of light. In an ideal world, the light of your brand would shine brightly and directly on your intended customers, so that they could see very clearly all the value that your brand offers them. But the clutter and the tumult of the marketplace crowd in between your brand and your customers, diffusing your light or obscuring it altogether.

Your company's stakeholders—partners, sales reps, service providers, community leaders, and influencers—also stand between your brand and your customers. In their roles they can distort the light of your brand—or they can help focus it. This is why brand building starts and ends inside your company. Brand initiatives should be undertaken to optimize all your stakeholders' roles and maximize the return on your investment in the brand. This is the function of the brand-as-business management approach, guided by the seven principles. When everything your stakeholders do is driven by your brand focus, your stakeholders will focus your brand's light on your customers with laser-like brilliance.

Perhaps the most distinguishing mark of the brand-as-business management philosophy is the way spending on the brand is viewed and handled. Traditional brand-building expenditures like advertising and public relations are considered a cost of doing business. As a result, they are managed as budget line items that often get cut when money gets tight.

With brand as business, money spent on the brand is banked as an investment in a core business resource. Dollars spent on building the business are dollars spent on building the brand, and vice versa. Delineating most brand expenditures as separate line items makes little sense once the brand investments are integrated into business plans, and business units are given responsibility for and are held accountable for brand development.

This is why great brands wait to communicate externally. They communicate after all the other elements of the brand have been developed and aligned, including product design. With a brand-as-business approach, Gap would have considered all the brand implications of its new product line before investing $130 million in promoting what turned out to be a giant flop. Likewise, Kodak's internal stakeholders would have gone the extra mile and sought to provide customers a fresh interpretation of "Kodak moments" for the new digital age.

As I write, the effects of the Great Recession linger on. Credit markets are tight and capital is scarce. It should be evident that former approaches to re-igniting growth and profits are unlikely to work in this climate. Technology, marketing, distribution, sales—none of these approaches will enable companies to achieve or sustain a market leadership position. Technology becomes a commodity very quickly. The public has grown tired of traditional marketing appeals. Intermediaries in distribution have grown adept at squeezing manufacturers' margins.

Even customer-centered approaches are not the answer, since large-scale enterprises can't possibly be all things to all people. And given the pace of change in today's business environment, success lies less in strategic planning and more in strategic decision making when opportunities arise. With a strong brand platform in place, it is much easier to make swift decisions that are consistent with all the values and attributes the company hopes to embody and deliver to customers.

For all these reasons, I believe that business leaders urgently need to adopt the brand-as-business approach described in this book. In uncertain times like these, brand as business has never made more sense.

For one thing, most business leaders are already frustrated by the often-wasteful expense that traditional branding strategies involve. These leaders should be curious, at the very least, about the way Zappos, Method, and Zara have all grown so fast on advertising budgets that are mere fractions of those of their competitors.

The great brands profiled in this book have higher-than-average profit margins in their respective sectors, which is hardly a coincidence. Consumers will pay a premium for products and services from great brands, especially those that manage to deliver on Principle Two, "Great Brands Avoid Selling Products," and Principle Seven, "Great Brands Never Have to 'Give Back.'" If you provide an emotional connection and a sense of identity in a way that is consistent with social and cultural consciousness, your customers will spend extra for the privilege of being one of your stakeholders. That's only possible with a brand-as-business approach to brand building.

If your company is doing fine right now, the urgent need for change might not seem obvious to you. Often when I'm speaking to CEOs and other business leaders, I find that many of the people who could profit from this message the most are also the most resistant to hearing it. The problem is that profitable companies are often blinded by their success and take their brand advantage for granted. And ironically, troubled companies, which are often short of both cash and goodwill among stakeholders, tend to view brand as business as a life raft when it may already be too late for them. The point I want to emphasize is that the time to change is now—not because your company is sick, but precisely because it is healthy.

CHAPTER 1

Great Brands Start Inside

Sam Palmisano was a twenty-nine-year IBM veteran when he took the reins of the beleaguered company as CEO in 2002. He had started as a salesman at IBM in 1973, but in the intervening years the IBM brand had lost its cachet and become seen as increasingly irrelevant.[1] The entire company nearly imploded during the 1990s, when almost half of IBM's 400,000 employees lost their jobs. "If you lived through this, as I did," Palmisano told *Harvard Business Review* in 2004, "it was easy to see how the company's values had become part of the problem."[2] The prized beliefs put forward by IBM's iconic founder—which included "respect for the individual" and "the pursuit of excellence"—had settled into a managerial culture of entitlement and arrogance. Palmisano determined to put the company on a new path by resetting IBM's stagnant, insular culture.

Palmisano's choice to change culture was hardly a typical move, especially at a company the size of IBM. The more common and attractive route for leaders in Palmisano's position is to overhaul the company's communication strategies—advertising, marketing, and promotions—and put a new fresh face on the company and its products. It's always easier to change what you say about your company than it is to actually change your company. Giving your image and message a public makeover is also the fastest way to get the attention of investors and customers alike. Conventional wisdom suggests that would have been the logical place for Palmisano to start rebuilding the IBM brand.

But what Palmisano recognized, as certain other visionary CEOs have, is that if you don't develop greatness among your employees, your employees are unlikely to deliver greatness to your customers. Clever advertising and a freshened-up logo will prove to be pointless exercises if cultural problems within the company prevent the company from delivering on its new promises. One of the fundamental ways an organization resets and strengthens its brand is through strengthening its culture. More than any other influence, company culture shapes the distinctive way employees behave as they turn the brand promise into breakthrough customer experiences.

Unless and until your culture is expressed clearly through your customer experience, you have nothing worth communicating. Your brand can't just be a promise; it must be a promise delivered. So your starting point is cultivating a strong internal corporate culture that aligns and integrates with your brand. Then you need to rally all your external stakeholders around those common cultural values. And finally you need to use your culture to optimize the company's operations and engage everyone who touches the brand in delivering a focused, unique customer experience. What follows is an outline of this three-step process and the tools and approaches that help great brands accomplish each step. When you can't see any daylight between what you believe, what you practice, what you offer, and what you say about yourself, you are doing what great brands do.

Putting Internal Brand Culture First

Modifying IBM's culture was particularly critical for Palmisano in 2002 because IBM's industry and market position were both undergoing significant change. The company had once been a computer hardware powerhouse, with software and business services playing second fiddle in its operations. By the time Palmisano took the CEO's chair, the two roles were reversed. The service side of IBM now produced the bulk of revenues and profits.[3] Palmisano had to lead the organization to meet the requirements of this new business model and he had to set expectations inside and outside the company for how his people would work—and ultimately succeed—within it.

As Palmisano noted, "When your business is primarily based on knowledge, [then] people—rather than products—become your brand. Just as our products have had to be consistent with the IBM brand promise, now more than ever, so do our people."[4] With more than 300,000 employees in 170 countries, Palmisano estimated that 40 percent of his workforce did not report daily to an IBM site—they either worked at client sites, from home, or were mobile.[5] Working from such far-flung locations with such low levels of direct supervision, employees would need what Palmisano called "a globally consistent set of values." He also knew that IBM's business scope would continue to change. "Managers come and go," he observed. "The business portfolio changes, so the only thing that endures is our culture."[6]

In July 2003, Palmisano used IBM's vast intranet communication network and collaboration software to initiate what he called a "ValuesJam." For seventy-two hours, employees all around the world were asked to riff on certain values themes that IBM executives had identified in a series of surveys and focus groups beforehand. The goal was to align every employee's daily focus with the values underlying the IBM brand. In Palmisano's words, "we needed to affirm IBM's reason for being, what sets the company apart."[7]

As with a musical jam session, the result was a discordant mix of inspiration and noise. The negativity and cynicism of some comments made them jarring to read, and at least one member of Palmisano's executive team wanted to cut the Jam short after eight hours. But Palmisano was determined to follow through on the promise of an unfiltered, uncensored seventy-two-hour exchange of ideas, because the process would ultimately help legitimize the end result. In the words of one IBMer who helped run the Jam, "If a bunch of execs go off in a closed room some-place, smoke a bunch of cigars and then emerge with some claim that this is what our values would be, it's going to be meaning-less." He added, "After all, Enron had a set of values."[8]

By the time the Jam had ended, fifty thousand IBM employees had logged in to read the debates, and ten thousand of them had left messages.[9] Palmisano took home a three-foot-high stack of documents that represented a cross-section of more than one million messages. IBM analysts used classification software to crunch all the postings and a small team was commissioned to work with the themes that emerged. The outcome of the process was three new interpretations of IBM's founding beliefs:[10]

- ◆ Dedication to every client's success.
- ◆ Innovation that matters—for our company and the world.
- ◆ Trust and personal responsibility in all relationships.

Most people would agree that these are good values for any workplace to have. Who would argue otherwise? But IBM imbued these values with much more importance. Palmisano called them "IBM's mission as an enterprise."[11] The values were intended to distill what IBM uniquely offers and delivers. As a result, IBM employees understood that these values describe what makes the IBM brand distinctive and valuable. Every company would like to have a strong workplace culture supported by inspiring values. With great brands, however, the culture and the values don't play supporting roles in business operations— culture and values *are* the brand, and they're used to inform business decisions and employee actions.

Making Culture Matter

The conversation about corporate culture that has recently flooded the pages of business books and journals has emphasized the need for a clear purpose and values. But true cultural change at your company hasn't occurred until all your employees, whether top leaders or field workers, are using your values to inform their daily behavior—with customers and with each other.

Culture building can't be simply *invertising*—internal communications efforts that treat employees as passive audiences who are expected to buy what the leadership or marketing team is selling. Feeling good about the organization and having a positive outlook on its future are important, but they're not likely to prompt changes in employees' design and delivery of customer experiences. Great brands use culture building to *educate*—to help employees understand what a brand is and why it's important. They use it to *define*— to explain what the brand stands for and how it is differentiating. They use it to *activate*—to help people understand their own impact on brand perceptions and therefore what is expected of them.

The challenge then becomes what I often call the "head + heart + hands and feet" problem. For your employees to understand, embrace, and deliver your brand, they need to know its values in their heads, feel inspired by them in their hearts, and then put them into action with their hands and feet. Processes such as IBM's ValuesJam and any number of other culture-building efforts are meant to engage heads and hearts. But values won't make a difference unless they stimulate changes in behavior—hands and feet.

Operationalizing your brand through company culture requires a focus on design, empowerment, and impact. You want to design the organization and its business model so it delivers on the brand values and attributes. You want to empower your people with the tools and resources to infuse the brand into their day-to-day decisions and behaviors. Finally, you want to make such a positive impact on your employees' lives and their careers that they support your brand's message and mission because they know their own destinies and your brand's destiny are intertwined. One mark of a great brand is that even former employees remain proud to say they helped make the brand great.

Enduring pride is just one of many benefits companies realize when they use their brands and their brand messages to increase employee engagement, rather than resorting to generic corporate initiatives. A brand is the strongest engagement tool a business has precisely because of its power to connect. Employees who are engaged with the brand:

◆ Connect to customers more effectively because they understand the value the company produces and delivers to them.
◆ Connect to each other more fully because they are united by a common objective and common set of values.
◆ Ultimately, connect to the brand's higher purpose and find that their work holds more meaning and importance to them because they see their own roles in the broader mission of the organization.

Brand engagement is in short supply these days. The Gallup organization asked more than three thousand randomly selected workers to assess their agreement with the statement "I know what my company stands for and what makes our brand(s) different from our competitors." Just 41 percent of employees strongly agreed with this statement, while 24 percent either disagreed or were equivocal. These results suggest that "too many companies are failing to help their workers understand what makes their company different and better than the rest," the report concludes.[12] And if your employees don't understand that, how can they help your brand achieve greatness?

◆ Tool: Using a Brand Toolbox to Ensure Brand Alignment

Method Products is a company that had started out with a freewheeling seat-of-the-pants culture driven by the purpose of crashing the multibillion-dollar household cleaner and detergent industry. But as co-founders Eric Ryan and Adam Lowry explained in their book, *The Method Method*, rapid growth posed a problem of how to preserve the company's magic without drowning it in workplace procedures and protocols.[13]

Ryan and Lowry raised the question with people at a handful of companies they admire, including Apple, Google, Pixar, Nike, and Starbucks. Three recommendations emerged from those discussions: Hire people whose personalities fit the existing culture, offer instruction in the culture from the start of their employment, and give all employees lots of feedback on what the company's values and culture really mean.[14]

A subsequent company-wide process defined Method's values as a "Methodology" of caring, collaboration, and innovation, topped off by two values that really distinguish the Method brand: "Keep Method weird" and "What would MacGyver do?" To help with the "head + heart + hands and feet" challenge, the company each year prints up a fresh deck of playing card–style flash cards that illustrate how the various values translate into explicit brand-building behavior—the card defining MacGyver-style resourcefulness reads "not accepting no for an answer" and "looking under rocks" for what others have missed.[15] Each deck of cards is bound by a key ring, so it's easy to share and can be hung on an employee's desk for easy reference.[16]

Without hands-on tools like the deck of flash cards, you run the risk of having employees who may truly believe in the values behind their brand but can't see the relevance of those values to themselves and their jobs. I frequently work with clients to build what I call a "Brand Toolbox" of content and decision guides to drive the approaches and behaviors needed to operationalize their brand values. The Brand Toolbox—developed over a period of months and published and distributed in a wide variety of ways including workbooks and downloadable PDFs, depending on the company communications style and infrastructure—informs managers and employees by communicating what the brand platform is and by providing principles to guide brand execution. It also inspires people with images, stories, and quotes. It gets them excited about the brand and motivates them to change their behavior in support of it. At its best, the Brand Toolbox instructs—it helps people make decisions and take actions that are "on brand" by including explicit instructions and clear-cut tools.

The contents of a Brand Toolbox depend on the specific needs of the company but usually a Brand Toolbox contains

- ◆ An explanation of your brand strategy along with background and rationale so that everyone can understand why you're doing what you're doing, and definitions of key terms so everyone grasps the meaning behind the words
- ◆ Principles and guidelines for delivering brand values and attributes at key touchpoints between your brand and the outside world
- ◆ Sample applications for how the brand should be expressed and delivered

◆ Guides that walk people through important decisions, along with outlines that map processes so that people learn how to do things on brand like select a co-marketing partner and screen a new product

What a Brand Toolbox is *not* is a brand standards manual or style guide—though you also need those documents that show how logos, fonts, and other elements of brand expression should be used. A style guide is important, but it's only that—it's about style. The Brand Toolbox is about substance. It's not about what you express; it's about how you execute. A well-designed Brand Toolbox that is properly used can unleash the power of your brand throughout your organization. The end result is one clear, consistent, common understanding of your brand among everyone who works on it.

Brand Toolboxes in Action

An insurance company I worked with included in its toolbox a "word bank" of key terms and phrases that helped convey the brand beyond the specific wording used in its strategic brand platform. For example, one of the company's core values is "passion that delivers results." The word bank suggested the use of similar positive terms such as inspired, effective, dedicated, overcomes obstacles, growth, success, visionary, leadership, wow!, energized, enlightened, tenacity, diligence, determination, commitment, persistence, resolve. This simple glossary of suggested terms helped everyone in the company develop a common language while representing the brand. Everyone—from receptionists to salespeople to service reps and right on up to the C-suite—could help ensure that the outside world would hear these positive values represented consistently and accurately in association with the company brand.

A major e-retailer used its Brand Toolbox to help web design-ers understand that the brand's chief cultural values were service and expertise, not low prices. The document included a diagram that showed how the competitive landscape was crowded with low-cost challengers and identified the ways in which the com-pany differentiated itself by truly adding value for customers. The resulting web page designs emphasized reviews, testimoni-als, comparison tools, product videos, and "you also might like" suggestions—all the functionality to help customers arrive at the perfect purchase, which embodied the brand's essence.

Even though your marketplace may change quickly, you want your culture and values to remain steady over time. A Brand Toolbox can help your company adapt to new opportunities by providing reinterpretations of its brand to fit the circumstances. When an upscale fitness retailer had to adjust to a larger market filled with less committed, less experienced customers, we knew that employees would have difficulty understanding these new customers and embracing how critical they were to the future of the company. So in the company's Brand Toolbox, a collection of downloadable documents and worksheets, we developed a set of compelling customer profiles with images, descriptions, and quotes to represent these new target customers that the brand now needed to appeal to.

In addition to outlining the standard demographic and cat-egory usage data for these customers, we painted pictures of their lifestyles and attitudes. One target segment included young people who liked to play in casual sports leagues and to work out with friends at the gym. We explained that these new customers wanted athletic gear that could be used for enhancing their fun in a wide variety of activities—very different from the current customers, who were mostly older and interested only in special-ized equipment that would improve their running performance. We showed pictures of the new breed of customers and included vignettes about them in a video demonstrating their desire for a lot of help and guidance from retail salespeople—again, very different from the sophisticated amateur athletes who had been shopping there for many years. We used the toolbox to inspire all employees about the new opportunities the new customers represented and to teach them how to adjust their decision making in product design, retail layout, customer service policies, promotions, and all the other functions of the company.

Most Brand Toolboxes are created and distributed in video and electronic documents, but some companies build websites and mobile applications to increase access and integrate interactive elements. When I was at Sony, we used a section of our web-based Brand Toolbox as a virtual bulletin board for employee discussions about the brand. We even held contests in which people submitted examples of ways they had operationalized the Sony brand in their work. Everyone who submitted an example was entered into a drawing with prizes that included a TV and a camcorder. Entries streamed in from all areas and levels of the company and some were really thoughtfully written stories, offering everyone a unique bonding experience of learning from each other's examples.

This was a case in which the medium *was* the message. The contest made it clear that the brand and the culture were things that everyone contributed to. We didn't want the only voices of brand alignment and engagement to be those of top executives. Culture building that comes across as too top-down can frustrate and alienate longtime veterans of the organization, denying the company the benefits of their wisdom and experience.

So many people had been at Sony for their entire careers. There was a lot of institutional pride and years of successes that we knew would serve as rich fodder for brand understanding. One longtime customer service representative wrote about her contribution to Sony's differentiation: "To my customers, I am Sony.

With the number of new players in this industry, quality customer service will be valued now more than ever. Letting the customer know you care and are truly interested in resolving their issue is demonstrating Sony is like no other." A person in the online demand generation group explained how he operationalized the brand values of innovativeness and imagination: "By not being satisfied with the way we have managed our programs in the past, or by the way our competitors conduct their online advertising, I can push the envelope and develop advertising units that showcase our products' unique features and applications." Another employee offered a helpful perspective on innovation, saying that it includes "innovative solutions to problems (such as creative solutions to supply chain issues) by being flexible and ready to change. Innovation is more than just in the way we design our products; it is a way of thinking." These and the many other submissions we received advanced the thinking and practice of brand building throughout the organization far more powerfully and convincingly than any executive edict would have.

◆ Tool: Increasing Brand Understanding Through Brand Engagement Sessions

Creating a Brand Toolbox is an important first step in fostering a strong brand culture, but the managers of great brands know that simply producing brand content and tools is not enough. They stage Brand Engagement Sessions featuring hands-on exercises and immersive experiences to ensure that brand understanding is followed with appropriate actions and decision making by their staff.

Brand Engagement Sessions should be held at all levels of the company, in all departments, across all functions. If yours is a large, complex, or multinational corporation, it makes sense to stage sessions with large divisions or groups and incorporate small breakout groups. For smaller, less distributed organizations, a series of department-by-department sessions may be more effective. Your first Brand Engagement Session is best conducted with your executive committee. By having your top leaders devote the time to really dig into the brand strategy and understand its implications, you ensure decision-making alignment at the highest levels of your organization and you set the stage for an effective rollout of Brand Engagement Sessions throughout the company.

Typically these sessions include a dynamic presentation of the brand platform followed by facilitated discussions, games, and interactive exercises. For example, when Starbucks rolled out its latest brand refresh, it staged a series of "brand days" for all its managers. It rented a warehouse and created a walk-through experience of the brand that followed the journey of coffee beans from the moment they are picked to the last stage of roasting. The smell and taste created an inspiring, visceral experience. Not only did the session present the brand in a tangible way but it explained the business case behind the changes.[17]

The right tone and agenda of your Brand Engagement Sessions depend upon your company culture overall and the specific group you're working with. For a high-energy creative session, you might plan a photo scavenger hunt in which groups photograph examples of brand touchpoints and take pictures of themselves demonstrating the brand attributes and values. Then each group assembles a collage of the photos with captions and headlines to explain the brand principles and presents it to other groups. A more content-driven approach might feature customer listening booths—phone-booth-like stations where people listen to recorded interviews with customers about their experiences with the brand. After employees visit the booths, you can ask them to share their reactions and ideas for how to improve the brand experience. One client of mine even ran a game show in which teams competed to answer questions about the brand platform, target customers, and company priorities.

The idea is to get employees excited about working on the brand and to help them identify decisions and behaviors aligned with the brand's message. By going beyond routine employee communications with interactive group experiences, you help connect people, brand purpose, and values in fun and memorable ways.

Brand engagement sessions also help address one point that is crucial to the brand-as-business model. In most organizations, it is a commonly held belief that brand building is solely the job of the marketing department. That's not the common understanding, however, behind great brands. One of the most important virtues of brand building *through* cultural change is that it impresses upon all employees that they each bear responsibility for interpreting and reinforcing the brand through their roles and in their daily decision making. That's the reason why every employee should participate in a Brand Engagement Session. Depending on your resources and other priorities, it may take up to a year to do a complete brand engagement rollout—and you may need to integrate the rollout into existing meetings and other programs. But the goal should be for everyone in the organization to share a common understanding of what the brand stands for and what constitutes the brand's defining values and attributes.

At Sony, where the image and perceived value of our brand had been so firmly shaped by strong national advertising, almost everyone assumed that brand building was marketing's exclusive domain. So we had to make a series of particularly strong and concerted efforts to communicate the exact opposite, that the Sony brand was everyone's business.

At a national sales meeting one year, we held a special "Being Sony" Brand Engagement Session for our salespeople, to help them understand their role in interpreting and reinforcing the brand. We sat people at tables in groups of six to eight and gave each group an electronic polling device. Then we conducted a quiz made up of questions about brands in general and the Sony brand specifically: What is the estimated financial value of the Sony brand? What is the definition of a "brand"? Which touchpoints have been proven to impact brand perceptions the most? For each question, the small groups had to debate and decide on an answer before entering it into the device. Results were displayed on a big screen along with the correct answer.

Salespeople are competitors by nature, so it wasn't long before a giddy competitive spirit developed in the room, and a huge cheer went up for the winning group. I knew we had accomplished our objective when, afterwards, one participant came up to me and said, "I never really understood what you meant by 'the Sony brand' until today."

Equipping and Empowering Your Employees

Brand Engagement Sessions can be used to equip groups or departments with the specific knowledge or experiences they need to operationalize the brand, or to engage them in working sessions to identify the strategies and programs they need to develop and implement to align their priorities with the brand. For a technology solutions company, we gathered the top 250 leaders for a "brand day" to align and engage them with the company's new brand platform. The day's agenda included a session titled "Models of Success," in which people worked in cross-functional teams to research several companies we wanted to learn brand-building best practices from. Each group was asked to note what the model company wanted its brand to stand for and what the company did to bring those values and attributes to life. Participants discovered insights about specific practices, policies, and programs, and identified the ideas they thought might be applicable to their company. As each group reported out the highlights of their discussion, it was clear participants had been inspired and challenged by these Models of Success.

Then, in what we called "Breakthrough Sessions," we gathered the participants by business unit and asked the functional groups to work together to identify how they could align their divisions' work and culture with the brand. We gave them specific questions to consider, and the resulting discussions were rich and rousing. We also challenged the leaders to each commit to one thing they would start doing to align with the brand and one thing they would stop doing, since we wanted everyone to leave that day with at least two tangible steps they could implement right away. These exercises laid the foundation for the participants to go back and run Brand Engagement Sessions with employees in their departments, and ultimately to spearhead brand-building strategies and programs throughout the organization.

When everyone in the organization is truly engaged with the brand, people naturally involve themselves in the development and delivery of brand value. From executive committee members to frontline employees, they can see themselves as "brand operators" who develop, maintain, and activate the brand across all of their activities. This serves as a point of pride and offers them a reason for increased commitment to the organization.

Evidence that your culture building is succeeding can be found in employee surveys designed to measure how well employees say they understand the brand strategy, how they rate the importance of the brand to the organization's success and to their own personal engagement with the company, and how much they claim to be applying the brand values and strategy in their daily decision making. Although these are self-reported measures, employees usually answer these questions honestly and accurately if the surveys are administered anonymously.

Participation metrics are another indicator of your progress. Track how many and which groups and levels of employees are participating in brand programs like contests and downloading and using resources like brand tools. You can also measure and monitor brand culture building by having the company's executive committee and other leaders conduct regular organizational assessments. They should assess the organization as a whole and discrete divisions or departments on how well their strategies and programs align with the brand and on the degree to which they integrate brand understanding into processes and use brand values in priority setting and ongoing decision making.

Extend Your Brand-Building Culture Externally

Internal alignment and integration is only one piece of the puzzle. Many other groups and people impact the brand experiences you deliver, so great brands also rally all external stakeholder groups around common cultural values that create unique, sustainable brand identities.

As I've said, if you were to conceive of your brand as a source of light, you'd want that light to shine as clearly and brightly as possible to show the outside world all the value the brand offers. Now think of all your stakeholders. The businesses your company works with to develop, make, distribute, and sell your product or service are powerful lenses through which your brand light is transmitted.

Great brand culture building extends beyond employees to external stakeholders because everyone who has a stake in your success has the opportunity to reflect and focus your brand message to the rest of the world. Your brand can be used to align and unify all these disparate efforts by explaining this is who we are, this is what we believe, and this is the value we deliver to customers. In fact, your brand forms the basis of your relationships with your stakeholders by defining the unique way you do business—your culture and the way you organize, recruit, train, motivate, manage, direct, negotiate with, and communicate with and about them. This is the ultimate functional benefit of the brand-as-business management approach. When everything your stakeholders do is driven by your brand, your stakeholders will help direct your brand's light to the outside world with laser-like brilliance.

A report by the *Gallup Business Journal* cautions against underestimating the power of brand alignment among those stakeholders who don't directly deliver products or services to your customers. They may be working behind the scenes but they are still key to your organization's ability to deliver on its brand promise. They must understand the core elements of your organization's brand identity and promise. They must also feel empowered to deliver them.[18]

Aligning Stakeholders

To these ends, brand initiatives should be undertaken to optimize all your stakeholders' roles and maximize the return on your investment in the brand. IKEA has done an exceptional job of extending its brand values to its thousands of global suppliers through something it calls "The IKEA Way" or "IWAY," which sets out a clear list of standards for everything from environmental practices to employee working conditions. What's important to note for our purposes is that the IWAY is not used by IKEA merely to burnish its reputation for being friendly to environmental and human rights efforts (although that is a likely side-benefit). For IKEA, the main purpose of IWAY is to extend its culture and maintain brand consistency, because environmental stewardship and good working conditions are values that help IKEA define its brand.[19]

What IKEA recognizes is that its business really is an ecosystem of many groups and companies, and its relationships with these other entities actually do form a set of vital partnerships in operationalizing the IKEA brand.

The list of partners in this sense includes vendors, strategic alliances, distribution channels, service providers, franchisees, affiliates, investors—even bankers have become brand stakeholders in the current credit-constrained business environment. Whether these partnerships are ongoing or one-time, amicable or adversarial, exclusive or not, these groups work with, on, and for the brand. As with employees, they can either build your brand or weaken it.

If these partners don't embrace your brand and align with your culture, your brand can be compromised. Just think how shoddy materials or shipment delays can ruin the experience a customer has with your brand. The increasingly common recalls of toys and tainted food have shown how seriously a brand can be damaged when a company's business partners fail to adhere to its standards. The actions of a shady sales rep or an incompetent service provider may yield less critical consequences, but they nonetheless reflect on your brand.

It's easy to take some stakeholder groups for granted. You can't assume that your advertising, media, and marketing agencies "get" your brand—nor should you limit their involvement with your brand by treating them simply as service providers or creative resources. They are brand stakeholders whose brand engagement needs to be actively nurtured and cultivated. If they don't understand and embrace the core values and culture of the brand, they're likely to pursue creativity over integrity, resulting in expensive efforts that interpret the brand inappropriately. If they are not familiar with how you are designing your brand experiences and engaging employees and partners to operationalize the brand, their campaigns may set up expectations that can't be met. That's why all agencies need to share one common understanding of the brand platform, and they must be aligned with you on what is on brand and what is not.

Other stakeholders who are often overlooked are your board members and key investors. By definition, these critical groups are profoundly invested in the success of your company, and if you find ways to engage them and enroll them in your brand culture, they can be among your company's greatest drivers of value creation. When you take the time to ensure they share your values, they will approve capital expenditures, hiring decisions, and M&As that advance your brand objectives. When they are engaged as ambassadors for your brand, they can bring credibility and drive positive coverage of your brand in the media.

Adapting Brand Tools for Stakeholders

For these and other stakeholder groups, you want to adapt the cultural engagement approaches you use with employees. Versions of the Brand Toolbox should be developed for the different stakeholder groups, with the content tailored to the appropriate level of detail. For example, your initial Brand Toolbox for employees might include customer profiles, while the version for your company's staffing service provider might emphasize employee profiles, outlining the character traits and personal values that successful employees share. A Brand Toolbox for your channel partners should include a deep dive into sales and marketing featuring customer acquisition strategies, sales playbooks, and pricing guidelines. For your advertising agency and marketing firms, you'll want to include detailed communications guidelines and examples, whereas these would not be necessary to share with your technology solutions provider.

I often hear concerns about sharing too much with external players, for fear of confidential information landing in the wrong hands. The truth is, in this day and age, there's really very little that others can't find out about you anyway. On the other hand, there's much to be gained by being open, transparent, and specific about your brand with outside stakeholders. That's why you should consider publishing and distributing brand tools as widely as possible. The rewards far exceed whatever risks are involved.

For these same reasons, Brand Engagement Sessions should be held with different groups of stakeholders and the content, format, and style should be tailored to each group. For example, I've found that suppliers often benefit from seeing "day in the life" videos of customers that show how they live and how they interact with the brand. Suppliers tend to operate at such a far remove from actual customers that they especially enjoy and learn from seeing how their work affects and benefits real people. Any way of giving suppliers a sense and feel of how customers respond to and value your brand can help them understand your culture and inspire them to contribute to it.

The engagement session for your advertising agencies might include a brainstorming session on how to bring the brand to life in creative programs. For other business partners, adapting a brand quiz about "how well do you know our brand?" might be a fun way to inform and inspire them about what your brand and its culture is really about. For your board of directors, perhaps you'd want to give a high-level presentation on the brand and then bring in an expert to facilitate a discussion about how the board can nurture and protect the brand, since an outsider can provide the neutrality that may be needed to engage external and internal board members in a discussion on a level playing field.

All these tools and activities help draw together everyone who works for or with your company in a common cultural bond, and with a common goal to create customer experiences that build your brand image and brand equity.

Culture Drives the Business

A vital, vibrant culture unifies, aligns, focuses, motivates, and propels all your company's stakeholders forward, but you still can't tell whether the culture change has truly taken root until the customers can feel it. With great brands, company culture and customer experience are inextricably linked.

It doesn't make sense for a company to develop purpose or values statements to inspire and engage employees if those statements aren't aligned and integrated with how the company inspires and engages its customers. A vibrant workplace culture is not enough.

Please don't misunderstand me. I am a huge believer in the importance of purpose, values, principles, and beliefs to organizations. But without the alignment and integration of culture and customer experience, at best you end up with employees who are well-meaning but don't produce the right results. At worst, you confuse employees as well as customers—and cause both groups to question your integrity.

Returning to the case of IBM, Sam Palmisano noted that the ValuesJam process had convinced everyone that there was plenty of agreement on the values behind the IBM brand. The debate then moved to the question of whether the organization could actually live up to those ideals in its interactions with customers. Palmisano first instructed all fifteen of his direct reports to start identifying gaps between the company's practices and its values. In very short order, they discovered all sorts of routine IBM procedures that obstructed IBM's value of "dedication to every client's success." For instance, managers complained that the need to get formal approval for even minor expenses often prevented them from solving customer problems quickly. After a pilot program proved the efficacy of giving frontline managers $5,000 of "discretionary walk around money," the program was expanded to all twenty-two thousand IBM frontline managers. Palmisano called it "a $100 million bet on trust." The program, he said, also helped prove to everyone "that we live by our values."[20]

The ability to execute on that kind of alignment of values is what distinguishes a great brand's culture from the rest. If you're like most business leaders, and you struggle with the gap between your brand strategy and how that strategy gets executed, you need to accept that company culture may be the weak link. Without strong cultural alignment, it's very easy for hardworking and talented people to work at cross-purposes and produce mediocre results because they all have different opinions about what's on brand and what's not. With disputes of that kind, the customer always loses. Delivering brilliant customer experiences depends upon having your employees' workplace values aligned with each other and with your brand.

Converting Culture into Customer Experience

For the brand culture to reach customers on a reliable basis, companies need to devote time, attention, and resources toward training and retaining a loyal base of frontline employees and managers. At the Wegmans grocery chain in the U.S. Northeast, cashiers are not permitted to interact directly with customers until they've gone through forty hours of training. Employees in special departments like meat and fish undergo ongoing training in their specialties. The chain sends store workers on trips around the country and even overseas to see firsthand where the food they are selling comes from and how it's produced.[21]

Company president Danny Wegman once told *Fast Company* magazine that these and other cultural measures are how Wegmans manages to stand up to Wal-Mart and other price-cutting competitors. The culture of Wegmans, he said, is "telepathic levels of customer service." Wegmans' cadres of loyal, well-trained, and knowledgeable store workers are "something our competitors don't have and our customers couldn't get anywhere else. . . . Anything that requires knowledge and service gives us a reason to be." Employees are happy to stand in the aisles and share with customers their expertise about meats and cheeses, for instance, because many have been flown at company expense to see these foods produced in Colorado, Argentina, Wisconsin, Italy, and France.[22]

It makes sense that culture drives the way the Wegmans brand distinguishes itself. "When you think about employees first, the bottom line is better," Kevin Stickles, Wegmans' head of human resources, told one reporter. "We want our employees to extend the brand to our customers."[23]

While Wegmans' spending on its employees and its brand culture may seem like an extravagance that few companies can afford, recall the survey research I referenced in the Introduction, telling how nearly two-thirds of chief marketing officers at major companies say that brand considerations do not influence decision making at those companies. That statistic suggests that billions of marketing and advertising dollars are squandered every year on the production and distribution of images and messages that do not square up with company culture and, in turn, customer experience. What is the resulting cost impact on customer loyalty lost to confusing and frustrating customers by sending them these mixed messages?

Mixed messages are a particularly serious problem in the fast food or quick-service restaurant industry, where consumer cynicism about advertising claims is widespread. Results from a survey research project I completed revealed that a full 48 percent of quick-serve customers see a big contrast between what they experience during visits to restaurants and what the advertising had promised. That's a severe disconnect that's liable to happen to any company that doesn't prioritize cultural change and brand alignment.

Ultimately it is culture that drives a brand's promise into operations, and then into customer experience. Again, IBM provides a case in point. One of the issues that emerged in the

ValuesJam was that IBM's complex system of internal pricing among its many units and divisions often made it slow or even impossible to give a prospective client a quotable price on an integrated, solution-oriented package of services.

Could these complex pricing problems have been cleared up without the ValuesJam? Palmisano was not so sure. "To be honest," he told *Harvard Business Review*, "we'd been debating the pricing issue at the executive level for a long time. But we hadn't done anything about it. The values initiative forced us to confront the issue and it gave us the impetus to make the change." ValuesJam and the resulting debates, he said, "were great inertia-busting vehicles."[24]

Execute First; Communicate Later

If you're like most of the business leaders I've shared these ideas with, you may be nodding your head in agreement and thinking, "Of course, our brand is not what we say, it's what we do." It's easy to agree with this sentiment—it's much harder to actually make it true.

Yes, cultural change is difficult. But there are other difficulties on the horizon that might make cultural change not a choice but an imperative. Customer expectations today are on a constant upward trajectory. People are becoming more knowledgeable and discriminating about their spending decisions. They're swayed less and less by slick salespeople and cool promotions and are forming their brand preferences more and more around what they actually experience when they do business with you and your company.

Democratization of information plays a huge part in this process. Consumers rely not only on their own experiences but on the experiences of your other customers, through the endless array of consumer review websites, mobile applications, and social media. If they buy from you, they in turn use these new tools to share their own opinions to influence others. In this environment, traditional sales and marketing tactics are becoming subordinate to customer experience, which is emerging as the most powerful form of marketing you can undertake.

Sam Palmisano's decision to work on IBM's culture first also signaled a choice to save communicating the brand message for later. Only after putting new services and solutions into place and ensuring that the culture was ready to support these fresh approaches did IBM move ahead with the launch of its "ON Demand" advertising campaign. By leaving marketing and advertising changes for last, IBM could use the campaign to express its cultural values of responsiveness, flexibility, and results without fear that customer experiences would undermine the credibility of the brand.

Author Jim Collins has cited Boeing's momentous decision to build the 707 airliner in the 1950s as an example of how big decisions should spring from a deep understanding and acceptance of the company's culture. Most companies start with the outside world and work on trying to adapt to it, Collins told an interviewer. "[But] greatness doesn't happen that way. It starts with an internal drive." In Boeing's case, Collins said, the company's core values included a spirit of adventure and an aspiration to greatness. The company was guided by its internal drivers. Only after cultivating its internal foundation, in the context of its unique culture, did Boeing take stock of how the outside world was changing (from military to civilian aviation, from propeller planes to jets), and how the company might contribute by doing what it does best—build a revolutionary jet airliner. "I believe that it is the internal imprint that drives all the action," Collins said. "Everybody harps about 'It's all about responding to the outside world.' But the great companies are internally driven, externally aware."[25] Great brands put culture first.

When you start brand building with brand communications, you're simply expressing your brand. But starting inside is about *executing* your brand. The rest of this book shows how great brands execute on their strong cultural foundations in every aspect of their businesses—from their high-level strategies to their detailed decision making. When you begin with reforming and recommitting to your company culture, your brand produces a direct and lasting impact on all areas of your business. This sets you on your way toward defining the emotions your brand embodies.

CHAPTER 2

Great Brands Avoid Selling Products

Just Do It" is one of the best-known advertising taglines of all time. But it's more than just a pithy phrase; it embodies the counterintuitive approach to brand building that underlies what great brands do.

In 1987, Nike's advertising agency had produced a new television spot for the company, one that celebrated Nike's early role in founding the jogging craze in America. Stunning visuals were shot at the University of Oregon running track where the first Nike shoes were developed. Clips of famous runners, including Steve Prefontaine (who died tragically at age twenty-five), were cut into the ad. "It started here," a voice intoned. "The Fitness Revolution that changed America."

The ad was meant to be striking and provocative, and it was. But when it was previewed before a crowd of more than a thousand sales reps at Nike's annual meeting, it was met with silence. That was not the inspired reaction company founder Phil Knight had hoped for. Shocked and feeling let-down by his ad agency, he sent them back to the drawing board. Nike's marketing chief at the time, Scott Bedbury, recalls in *A New Brand World* that the problem with the ad was that it celebrated Nike and its products, not the customer. "It was," Bedbury writes, "probably the best example of corporate navel-gazing ever produced."[1]

Two weeks later, equipped with a memo from Bedbury that asked them to "widen the access point" for Nike customers, the Wieden+Kennedy agency returned with a series of simple ads that showed athletes of all kinds doing what athletes do—sweating, straining, running, and jumping. There was an ad with a female triathlete. There was one with an eighty-year-old distance runner. Another featured a pro basketball player. All of them spoke with emotion about what they do, and why they do it, followed by the on-screen invitation: "Just Do It." As Bedbury writes, "'Just Do It' was not about sneakers. It was about values. It was not about products; it was about a brand ethos."[2]

The "Just Do It" ad campaign ran for ten solid years and serves as a prime example of how selling emotion triumphs over selling products. Rather than tell you how Nike products offer you superior performance and breakthrough innovation, Nike allowed the athletes—pros and amateurs alike—to tell you about the emotional rewards themselves, in their own highly emotional words, without ever mentioning Nike. As soon as the ads first came out, people called and wrote Nike to share how the tagline inspired them to "just do it." They told how they took up fitness, quit bad jobs, left bad relationships, and were otherwise inspired to change their lives by that three-word emotional appeal. In the years since the campaign launch, "Just Do It" has taken on a cultural resonance that remains unique among brands. To this day, people get tattoos that say, "Just Do It."

We humans are emotional creatures. We make our purchase decisions based on how products promise to make us feel. That's why great brands succeed by seeking intimate emotional connections with customers. Either the product satisfies an emotional need I have ("I want to feel healthy and successful") or it offers me access to a self-identity that I want to experience and express ("I'm an athlete").

Product features are usually of secondary importance to these emotional connections, and managers of great brands plan and take action accordingly. They first shape their brand identities with emotional values that differentiate their offerings and connect with consumers, and use product efficacy only to support those values. They then prioritize long-term customer relationships over short-term sales because they know customers who are emotionally connected to a brand are more valuable. And finally they use their brands—not product categories—to scope and scale their businesses. Their focus on emotional connections fuels product innovations and brand extensions. Moreover, they constantly address the question, What business are we really in? Nike, in this instance, made the fateful choice to not be a running shoe brand, and instead it entered a broader, more resonant class of inspiring people to become who they hope to be. Through this type of commitment to create emotional connections, great brands are always redefining consumer expectations and challenging the traditional norms of their industry categories.

Emotions Trump Efficacy

Few companies are as disciplined in linking products to emotions as Nike. Many of Nike's competitors try to beat Nike's products on the basis of innovation and style. But Nike's success has much more to do with its focused use of athlete relationships and innovative brand experiences to inspire its customers to feel like athletes. Its products and technologies are always linked to values such as aspiration, achievement, and status.

Most Nike products are functionally cool and technologically advanced enough, but the story Nike sells is the entrancing factor. "Nike is more than performance," Heather Amuny-Dey,

Nike's design director for North America says. "Nike is also about how we live. Nike focuses on innovation, style, story, and experience to create the emotional connection."[3]

The ethos that produced "Just Do It" is the ethos Nike continues to pursue today. All you have to do is compare its 2012 London Olympics ads with those of Adidas, a chief competitor. Adidas ran high-energy, fun spots that highlighted its products. Nike's commercials, by contrast, were quiet and moving. They made an emotional connection through a new call to action: "Find Your Greatness." It's no small wonder that the Nike's ads generated fifteen times as many Internet conversations as did the Adidas ads, even though Adidas had paid $155 million to be official Sportswear Partner of the Olympics.[4]

In this century, emotional brand building requires you to develop a personal dialogue with your customers on the issues that are most meaningful to them. Herbert Muschamp once observed (in a *New York Times* essay on product design), "[In] the last 50 years, the economic base has shifted from production to consumption. It has gravitated from the sphere of rationality to the realm of desire: from the objective to the subjective, to the realm of psychology."[5] Muschamp's point was that in a postindustrial society, material satisfaction is so easily attained that emotional fulfillment is now the true challenge for providers of goods and services. The key purchase question has moved away from "What does it do?" and toward "How does it make me feel?"

Even in business-to-business categories, emotions are highly influential. Despite the many warnings, businesspeople still rely on their guts more than their heads. RFPs are issued and vendor rosters are developed based on respect and risk-aversion—both emotional considerations for buyers. Managers make statements about themselves and their values whenever they select a supplier, expressing "I am an innovative thinker," "I am a respected authority," or "I am an aggressive risk-taker," depending on their desired identity.

In our commercial landscape, brand power is no longer driven by product efficacy. Instead brands form strong customer bonds through developing mind share and heart share, and to accomplish those ends, only emotive propositions will resonate. This is true today and it will likely be even truer tomorrow. The rising generation of Millennials, for instance, is not just looking for tasty treats at a good value when it comes to restaurant choices. In the estimation of one food industry research firm, Technomic, what Millennials want is much more complex: an emotional connection to a brand that is socially responsible and sustainable.[6] If they feel this way about fast food, just imagine their demands when making more consequential purchases. These consumers of tomorrow expect brands to inspire them and express their values so well that being a customer should be a source of pride and joy for them.

In essence, you want your brand to be *tattoo-worthy*. Or you want to ask yourself why it isn't.

Connecting Through More Than Category

Pampers was Europe's top-selling disposable diaper brand in 1997, but it was rapidly losing market share to Huggies. Somehow, Pampers as a brand was failing to connect with consumers, which baffled executives at parent company Procter & Gamble because Pampers really was the superior diaper. Their tests showed it was a marvel of product engineering that kept baby bottoms drier.

When Pampers marketers convened focus groups to study the problem, they soon discovered that dryness wasn't really the ultimate benefit that young mothers wanted from their babies' diapers. The deepest concern expressed by the mothers was for their babies' health and development. Dry diapers were important, but for reasons that Pampers' marketers hadn't fully appreciated: dry diapers allow babies to sleep better, and sound sleep addressed the mothers' fundamental emotional concerns about their babies' well-being and development.

In his book, *Grow: How Ideals Power Growth and Profit at the World's Greatest Companies*, former Pampers brand leader Jim Stengel writes that this insight sparked the beginning of a long road of transformation for Pampers. "Over time," Stengel recalls, "the organization morphed from a narrow focus on product benefits to a broad focus on delighting moms and enhancing their babies' development." One simple, practical step was to change the names of the diaper sizes in order to signal Pampers' concern for children's developmental stages: Swaddlers for infants, Cruisers for toddlers, and Pull-Ups for toilet training. In a more substantial change, design engineers who worked on Pampers were instructed that improved dryness was no longer their ultimate goal. The new measure of success was how well babies slept, which required the engineers to focus more on studying comfort, fit, and texture.[7]

Eventually, Pampers created a new ideal for itself as a brand that would partner with parents throughout their baby's stages of physical, social, and emotional development. A profound cultural change at Pampers resulted, very much in line with the "Great Brands Start Inside" principle outlined in Chapter One. Pampers' physical office setting was changed to reflect the new brand ideal. It was redecorated with baby-friendly color schemes, and mothers of newborns with their babies were brought in regularly to visit with employees. Maternity parking and in-house day care services were added to the premises, as well. On the Internet, Pampers was one of the first brand websites to offer a trove of useful advice and medical information—all devoted to the brand ideal of healthy babies and happy mothers. Pampers also went on to partner with UNICEF in a worldwide vaccination campaign to eradicate mother and child tetanus infections—its first tie-in ever with a social cause. Consumers responded to Pampers' new emotional connections with them, and global revenue grew from $3.4 billion in 1997 to $10 billion by 2001.[8]

Learning from Anthropology

It takes a lot of careful listening to arrive at insights that have the power to transform a brand as big and established as Pampers. Deciphering what people find most important emotionally necessitates playing connect-the-dots between what is said, why it's said, and how it's said—and what is not said. Traditional market research methodologies are limited in this respect. Focus groups and surveys usually rely on people to report on their attitudes and behaviors, but consumers are notoriously inaccurate in the information they provide. Most critically, they rarely get to their own underlying drivers for decision making—their emotions.

To dig beneath the surface with customers and develop keen market insights, it's necessary to borrow techniques from the realm of the social sciences. Research methods based on anthropology allow you to interpret meanings and values that underlie expressed attitudes and behaviors. Methods derived from the related field of ethnography rely on up-close, personal experience, participation, and observation on your part, so you can see how people unconsciously interact with your brand. Another discipline, empathic research, is useful because it calls upon you to put yourself in customers' shoes to understand the way they live and experience your products.

Particularly valuable anthropological methods include the in-home visit and the shop-along. By observing and interviewing select consumers in situ, where they are most comfortable and their behaviors are less censored, you are more likely to uncover their unspoken—and in some cases unconscious—needs and desires.

For a nutritional supplement manufacturer, I recruited customers who allowed my client and me to observe them using the product at home. Through the exercise we learned that some people felt so proud of being a brand user that they displayed the product canister on their kitchen countertop. That was not only for convenience. It served as a reminder that they were making smart choices for their health. It satisfied the emotional need, to signal to themselves and to visitors they were pursuing a healthy lifestyle.

That insight helped the client company reframe what it was selling. It wasn't nutrition. It was a healthy lifestyle, a much richer emotional terrain to navigate. In the shortest term, the shift in focus prompted a complete redesign of the product packaging. Previously the package had been cluttered with all sorts of the nutritional info and health claims. Now we simplified the message to the single claim of one hundred calories per serving, and we incorporated brighter colors, a crisper logo, and updated product images to make it more attractive for display on kitchen counters. In other marketing messages, we communicated how multiple health benefits were gained from making the smart decision to use this one single product. Finally we focused the product assortment on twelve-ounce canisters instead of two-pound jugs. Why? Because buyers would be more likely to keep the smaller package visible and accessible on all those kitchen counters.

◆ Tool: Discovering Insights at the Moment of Truth

A study for a fast food client borrowed more from ethnography to get at the emotions that determine a lunch destination. We did ride-alongs in which we studied office workers from the perspective of their unique tribal culture. The experiences revealed how people with time constraints and traveling in groups tend to navigate group dynamics, often by settling for a second-choice

compromise so as to satisfy everyone's needs. Our media advertising, we found, had little or no persuasive power in these situations. In fact, the ability to avoid making a left turn across a busy
street was far more important in choosing a lunch destination
than any advertising message.

These and other insights about the "the moment of truth" in
choosing a lunch spot prompted us to adjust the menu to provide
enough variety that we would avoid a veto from one party member. Store signage changed to reinforce the mass media advertising, which promoted new full-priced menu items. Previously we
had focused most of the outdoor signage on discounted products
and promotional messages, since we figured we had covered the
top-tier items in our advertising.

The ride-alongs resulted in changes in the substance of the
advertising, too. We shifted the message away from the quality
or the novelty of our product ingredients and instead conveyed
more of the crave-ability of the products—a more emotionally
resonant message. We realized that if we wanted people to con-
vince their workmates to visit our restaurant, we had better be
offering food that they felt they must have. After all, we found
that drivers had an often decisive urge to pick whatever restaurant was most convenient on the right-hand side of the road. We
needed people to be driven to satisfy their cravings if we wanted
to motivate them to make a left-hand turn against traffic just to
get to us.

More than anything, the ride-alongs helped persuade us that
demographics alone were not a useful segmentation strategy for
fast food restaurants. To make an emotional connection with any
customer, it follows that you should segment the market in a way
that is *needs-based*, and connect with prospects at the moments
when those needs are greatest. The best way to address fast food
customers would be on the basis of needs-based usage occasions:
"the don't-have-to-think-about-it quick bite when on the go,"

"socializing with friends and family" or "craving a particular menu item." Those were the segments that helped shape our strategies, not the usual demographic segments broken down by age and income. Age and income cannot help you fully anticipate and satisfy emotional needs. Needs-states can. (See Chapter Four to learn how to identify customer needs-states.)

◆ Tool: Using Empathic Research to Gain an Edge

By putting you in close contact with the private lives of your customers, empathic research helps you see your product through the eyes of someone with values, concerns, and emotional triggers that are different from your own. This perspective becomes absolutely critical when you are dealing with products that are highly personal—like photographs. So when I worked on a project involving the design and marketing of digital cameras during my time at Sony, empathic research on how the camera and its pictures were used became absolutely vital to our success.

We conducted the research in the late 1990s, when people were just starting to use digital cameras and camcorders. We approached the project with a lot of preconceived notions about picture taking. For decades, images were about preserving memories. They were used to remind people of important occasions in the past—weddings, birthdays, and so on. You'd set up the scene, take the picture, get it developed, put it in a nice frame on the mantel, and leave it there for years.

By watching and interacting with early users—people who had started using digital cameras well before they hit the mainstream—we learned that pictures were starting to play more of a role *during* the occasions and a more casual role at that. People would snap informal pictures in the middle of the action and share them with people right on the spot, using the instant display on the back of the camera. Picture taking and picture sharing added to the fun and action of the occasion in the moment.

They wouldn't be the best quality pictures and oftentimes people would take several pictures of the same shot—but now that they were free and disposable, getting the perfect picture was no longer as important. Sometimes images would then be saved, printed, and displayed, but many would remain in the camera forgotten after the moment passed.

This kind of behavior had not been anticipated by our product designers. They had assumed, as most of us had, that digital cameras represented a new, more convenient method of gratifying old, reliable emotional needs—to preserve memories of special occasions by putting images in photo albums and hanging them on walls. Many of our efforts had been focused on helping people take high-quality pictures and on transferring image files from camera to computer for printing and storage.

Instead, digital technology had opened up new opportunities to satisfy other emotional needs, like feelings of belonging and sharing *during* those special occasions. Our technology hadn't been addressing those needs. In some ways, it had thwarted and frustrated them. The instant displays on the backs of the cameras were small and functional, with low picture resolutions. The user interface for reviewing the photos was needlessly cumbersome. Finally, the cameras themselves could have been smaller, but few of us had foreseen how the usefulness of the cameras as a source of spontaneous fun would be enhanced if the size were reduced.

All the improvements you saw in Sony's digital cameras during the decade of the 2000s—larger, brighter instant displays, easy gallery-style browsing, wireless instant sharing options, and ever smaller camera sizes—were spurred by these kinds of empathic insights into how people felt about cameras and about photographs. It's important to understand that we weren't just trying to make Sony cameras better, and we weren't relying on surveys to tell us that consumers liked bigger displays and wireless transfers (although we did that, too). We watched and listened as these pioneering customers used our cameras. We heard them when those products failed to satisfy their emotional needs for spontaneous fun. Empathy also helped us understand why our products weren't more successful. Our cameras were loaded with excellent features but we had designed and marketed them with the intention of satisfying a completely different set of emotional needs, those of memory preservation. By focusing on promoting product features we had missed the emotional connection.

Emotional Brand Building for Long-Term Customer Relationships

Customers now expect to interact personally and deeply with companies, and with each other. Great brands are always engaged in relationship building—seeking long-term customer loyalty, retention, and satisfaction to generate a continuing revenue stream from existing customers. Emotional brand building focuses on the long-term customer relationship and encourages connectivity and intimacy.

In recent years, marked by a recessionary climate, many companies have followed the opposite tendency and emphasized transactional sales, in which the main objective is to maximize the return on each individual transaction. Everything becomes focused on immediate value delivery and short-term revenue generation. In the guise of relationship building, companies resort to punch-card-type loyalty programs, which, because they rely on reduced prices, don't really make the kind of emotional connection that builds relationships. These companies also tend to overcommunicate once they have your e-mail or mailing address, and you get the message: They are not interested in building a relationship with you. They are only trying to sell you something.

This kind of highly transactional marketing during slow business cycles would seem to make sense on the surface. When revenue is hard to find, you've got to work harder to generate it. But the truth is that when demand decreases and spending becomes restrained, there are fewer new transactions to be had. Great brands tend to win out during dry spells precisely because they are always engaged in relationship building. They are more likely to reward existing customers with special offers and less likely to engage in transaction-oriented "teaser rates" or "introductory rates" for new customers. They also are more likely to provide value-added services, not because they hope to raise revenue directly from the activity but because they know it will form a more valuable relationship for both parties down the road.

Consider how Amazon offers its users an open forum for customer reviews—good and bad—along with third-party listings of recommendations. When Amazon launched the review policy, founder Jeff Bezos had to agree with critics who said that bad reviews likely hurt Amazon sales. But, as Bezos told an interviewer, he believed Amazon "would make a lot more sales in the long term if we helped the customer make purchase decisions, and one of the ways we can help customers make purchase decisions is to allow customers to make negative reviews."[9]

Later, with the introduction of the Kindle Fire, Amazon probably took a hit to its short-term earnings; at any rate, technology experts believe the tablet reader has been sold at a loss. Amazon CFO Tom Szkutak had this to say about Amazon's strategy in an earnings conference call in 2012: "As we think about the lifetime value, we're thinking very specifically about the device itself, how to make sure that we get the absolute best device in customers' hands and have the absolute best content on those devices."[10]

Szkutak's point is that if the company could demonstrate to customers Amazon's unique brand proposition through a superior experience and gain people's trust and preference for the brand, the company would make up the difference in profitability through sales of e-books and other products on the tablet. Amazon is thinking beyond products and extending its brand to a brand ecosystem of services and content to which customers will remain emotionally connected for the long term.

Connections That Last

Emotional connections of this kind produce strong bonds of loyalty because customers begin to feel the emotional "switching costs" involved in trying out a competitor. Although most switching costs are monetary (think of cellular service contracts with high fines for early termination), making a switch involves psychological and emotional costs as well. Once someone feels a personal and meaningful bond with a brand, they're less likely to trade that relationship off—just as is the case in person-to-person relationships.

Those who identify with a brand and its products and services are more likely to urge others to switch to that brand. When people love your brand, they become your evangelists, your brand ambassadors. Ravi Sawhney of RKS Design wrote recently that there are two prerequisites for people's willingness to recommend a brand or experience. "First, there must be a strong level of emotional engagement, and second, they must feel their identification strongly represented or actualized (Does it complete me, or the "me" I wish I were?)"[11]

At that level of emotional engagement, consumers with close ties to your brand will respond to negative information about you as though they were being personally attacked—they feel the negativity as a threat to their self-image. According to one study by Tiffany White at the University of Illinois, brands become highly symbolic of consumers' self-concepts—so much so that consumers will defend their self-connected brands much as they would defend themselves from personal failure.[12]

Emotionally connected consumers are as motivated to protect the brand as they are themselves, observed White. "Consumers are highly resistant to brand failure to the point that they're willing to rewrite history." This explains the reaction of Toyota customers after the brand experienced some highly publicized recalls a few years ago, she says. They ignored the news and came to the company's defense in an effort to ensure a more positive brand story for the history books.[13]

A strong brand fosters brand loyalty—not only with increased repeat purchases, lower price sensitivity, or increased purchase frequency, but also in terms of protection when things go wrong—because in this day and age, it's not a matter of if something will go wrong, it's a matter of *when*. An emotionally engaged customer base may be the strongest defense you can wage in a PR crisis.

Expanding Your Brand Footprint Through Emotion

Powerful as emotional appeals were for Pampers and Amazon, such appeals drive even more than product optimization and brand loyalty. They're the fuel behind brand innovations and extensions.

In fact, one of the great advantages of having the kind of connection that great brands have with consumers is that they are less dependent on the appeal of any particular product. When we buy Nike products, for example, we're not buying shoes, shirts, and other gear. We're buying a dream. As a purveyor of dreams, Nike enjoys the flexibility to introduce new products and reinterpret its brand values through them.

The Nike+ line of products, including a Bluetooth-enabled wristband accelerometer, captures user performances and uploads data to a Nike+ website where users can track their progress online. "This kind of deeply immersive and connected product essentially becomes the company's de facto marketing," Nike's vice president of digital sport, Stefan Olander, told *Adweek*.

He observed that the brand engagement people now have is much more powerful than what could be achieved through communications. For each consumer, "It's an emotional connection to myself, and my achievement, and my friends."[14]

Extensions of this kind are only successful when your brand already has established a deep emotional bond with customers. Think for a moment about a different "bond"—James Bond. The brand that is James Bond maintains such a durable emotional connection with its audiences that the "product"—the actor playing James Bond—has changed seven times in the course of twenty-three films made in fifty-one years.[15] Fans of today's Bond might look back at early Bond movies from the 1960s and find them flat and cartoonish, because audience expectations have changed and become more sophisticated. But even though the old Bond is almost unrecognizable when compared with today's Bond, if you were to view the twenty-three Bond pictures in their order of release, you would see the gradual development of the Bond brand ethos—that sexy, witty calm in the face of mortal danger, always in the service of saving the world from destruction. The brand has evolved over time, changing the product continuously while maintaining the Bond brand's essence.

Nike is now undergoing a similar evolution, with a transformation so profound that it even impinges on Nike's iconic tagline. Olander explained, "People now demand us not to say, 'Just Do It,' they say 'Help me just do it.' 'Enable me to just do it.'"[16] Nike's brand identity remains one of inspiration, but that is now evolving from "inspiration through enrollment" to "inspiration through empowerment." With Nike+, the company is managing to do with fitness what Apple did with iTunes—sustain and build an ongoing relationship and emotional connection with its customers. Having long ago cemented a brand identity that was not confined by products, Nike enjoys the freedom to stretch into new product categories, including technology services and solutions.

At their best, great brands are always redefining consumer expectations and challenging traditional industry category norms. Managers of great brands constantly address the question, What business are we really in? to drive the development of innovative concepts that break category boundaries while maintaining their critical emotional ties to consumers.

Google is the world's dominant online search engine, but that does not begin to describe Google's answer to What business are we in? Google's stated mission, "To organize the world's information and make it universally accessible and useful," suggests a much more far-reaching scope.[17] With such an all-encompassing view of its brand potential, Google has launched the development of products as varied as a virtual wallet, Android phone software, the global Streetview project, and even a Groupon-type daily deal offering. This constant experimentation to identify new opportunities has also yielded its share of duds, including Google Voice Search, Google catalogs, and Google Answers. But by all accounts the company manages to maintain a creative culture by celebrating these failures as the inevitable result of its larger commitment to make deeper, richer, stronger connections with consumers.

With the exception of Richard Branson's Virgin-branded companies, no other brand has broken into so many different industries as Google. By refusing to limit itself to narrow categories of product lines, Google leverages its elastic brand equity to push the boundaries of possibilities in pursuit of new ways to connect with consumers. By applying its values and focusing on making connections grounded in emotions instead of products, Google opens up entirely new ways of doing business, as evidenced by the company's acquisitions of mobile device manufacturer Motorola Mobility and social advertiser Wildfire Interactive.

Amazon has grown in a somewhat similar way, out of a slightly narrower mission, to be "Earth's most consumer centric company; to build a place where people can come to find and discover anything they might want to buy online." Amazon's forays into home video streaming subscriptions and other entertainment offerings might seem surprising to someone who sees Amazon as an online bookstore—and fails to see Amazon as Amazon sees itself.

What Business Is Your Brand In?

Google and Amazon are striking cases of cash-rich companies with seemingly endless appetites for growth. But they demonstrate what great brands do and have set today's standard for how to question the true purpose of one's business, a practice that every business should emulate. Are fast food brands in the drive-through business or are they in the good-food-fast business? Are airline companies in the transportation business or are they in the business productivity business? Is the U.S. Postal Service in the mail-and-shipping business or is it in the connected-communities business?

Chapter One described how IBM was forced to confront this very issue, but only after it had laid off almost half its workforce. To transform itself into a software and service company, IBM had to reimagine its purpose and shed its old brand identity as International Business *Machines*. Many companies—and even entire industries, most famously the old railroads—either failed to make such a transformation or never even tried.

Theodore Levitt's provocative article, "Marketing Myopia" (first published in 1960), is one of the most reprinted articles in the history of *Harvard Business Review*. In it, Levitt argued that "every major industry was once a growth industry . . . but the reason growth is threatened, slowed, or stopped is not because the market is saturated. It is because there has been a failure of management."[18] His observation, made more than a half-century ago, is more relevant today than ever.

Sometimes the blinkered managerial mentality Levitt wrote about can be observed as reflected in the responses from industries being invaded by aggressive competitors such as Google, Amazon, and Apple. The typical reaction is for the besieged companies to defend their superior positioning in the market and their depth of expertise, when what they really should be doing is reviewing their company cultures, inspecting their connections with their customers, and reconsidering their reasons for being. In other words, they should be exploring the full potential of their brands and asking themselves, What business is our brand in?

When Apple came out with the iPhone in 2007, an executive with the Australian wireless company Telstra criticized Apple with this memorable assertion: "There's an old saying—stick to your knitting—and Apple is not a mobile phone manufacturer, that's not their knitting." Today the iPhone provides Apple with half of its revenues and an estimated two-thirds of its profits. Telstra is still around, but it's not too melodramatic to point out that bankruptcy courts are filled with companies that merely "stuck to their knitting" with a narrow product view of their brands when competitors moved in.[19]

So that would seem to be the surest way for a business to fail—to keep doing what it knows how to do, all the way to the bitter end. The truth is a little more complicated. It's just as easy to fail by attempting a transformation and then botching it. To fail to identify the correct opportunity, to fail to engage one's ability to exploit it, to give up strength, to expose a weakness, to underwhelm—all can be fatal, as well.

◆ Tool: Mapping Your Brand

The difference is usually attributable to understanding how to reframe your brand identity through emotional connections. And the best way I know of guiding the development of new products and breaking down walls between industry categories is to draw up a "Competitive Landscape Map" of your brand.

You begin by creating a chart with x and y axes and then plotting the relative positions of your brand and its competitors. Charts of this kind are tools managers commonly use to visualize their competitive positioning, but a well-conceived map can be much more revealing. A map, robust and astutely designed, can help you redefine what business you're really in and who your real competitors are.

The most critical decision to make in creating such a map is establishing the x-y values—the axes—that will best serve you in breaking new ground. You might need to experiment with several different maps before you find one that sparks real insight. The risk of not doing so is that if you default to very standard category variables such as the price:value axis (more expensive premium pricing versus less expensive value pricing), you may not learn very much.

Imagine the challenge facing a snack food company I worked with, where common competitive landscape x-y values might be price:value, sweet:salty, individual:shareable, kids:adults. We began one such project by using the anthropological research methods described earlier in the chapter. We spent several weeks getting to know our customers before we even considered what the x-y axes on our map should be. Snacking, after all, is not simply about putting food in your body.

Our test consumers were given journals and asked to keep track of all their different eating or snacking occasions over the course of several days. We asked them to note what they ate, the circumstances in which they ate, and how they felt before and after eating. We noted that the feelings they recorded were not just physical ones ("I feel hungry") but also emotional ones ("I'm lonely," "I'm excited"). We also saw the links between daily events, behavior, and feelings. The granola bar during the morning commute was about getting pumped up for work. The late-night snack after a hard day's work was a soothing indulgence. We saw plenty of evidence of people self-medicating their feelings with food.

The journals were supplemented with one-on-one interviews conducted by a cultural anthropologist who probed our subjects' psyches and value systems. He asked questions such as "How do you relate to people when you're hungry?" "How do you relate to them when you are full?" We ended up with twelve different consumer *demand spaces*—consumers' reasons and occasions for having a snack. They included some simple functional purposes such as "to tide me over" and "to supplement my diet" and a few more that were particularly revealing on an emotional level: "to treat myself and indulge" "to enliven a social occasion," and "to relax and unwind."

Out of all that research, we rooted out what we felt was a novel but important dimension of purchase influence: *emotional satisfaction*. This was something hinted at by consumers, but it was generally unspoken or unrealized by most of them. It so happened that emotional satisfaction was also well-aligned with the client's brand identity, so it was a strong area of opportunity. Our analysis of the data told us that most people typically assumed they faced a clear-cut trade-off when selecting a snack: They could satisfy a craving (and feel somewhat guilty that the snack was bad for them) or, alternatively, they could choose to eat something healthy (which wouldn't satisfy their craving, but they would feel good about themselves for having made a good choice).

So we constructed a Competitive Landscape Map that put "healthier choice:less healthy choice" on one axis and "emotional well-being:physical fulfillment" on the other. With this simple step, our research broke us clear of the boundaries of traditional snack food categories. The dimensions of our map were so broad that it included a far wider range of competitive product

Figure 2.1   Traditional Competitive Landscape Map

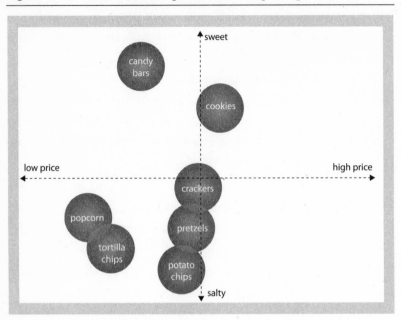

categories than we ever would have considered if we had only been looking at price or taste. (See Figure 2.1 for how the snack food category might have been mapped in a typical approach, and Figure 2.2 for how our methods led to a unconventional map that revealed a host of new product opportunities.) Our research had shown that when attending to their emotional satisfaction, consumers consider many different items as snacks—from nuts to cheese—many of which are far outside the standard industry definition of "snack food."

The most important point the map revealed was that although this field of snack competitors was enormous, only a few products and brands existed at the time in the upper right-hand quadrant of the map—the "healthier choice/emotional well-being" region. And of the few that were there, none of them had the high brand recognition or wide distribution that my client's products enjoyed. So we zeroed in on that space as the optimal position to

Figure 2.2 New Competitive Landscape Map

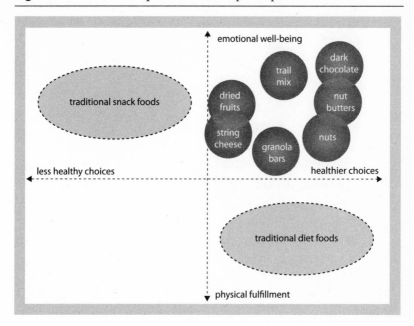

move the brand. The map eventually led to new ideas for snack items, new promotional strategies, and new communication approaches, all centered around the newly defined brand ethos of a healthier snack choice, using simple, pure ingredients, that is emotionally fulfilling.

This example illustrates how brands—not product categories— should be used to scope and scale a business in a competitive environment. It is brand research that enables a company to develop deeper, richer, stronger connections with customers and sustain their claims to strong and differentiated value propositions. Simply promoting "new and improved" products doesn't resonate as strongly with consumers nor does it sustain a competitive advantage.

By understanding the underlying emotions behind product perceptions and usage occasions, we were able to identify and develop a powerful brand positioning—then we developed our product line-up to fill it. And although the mapping process itself took just three to four months, the execution on the plan we devised took several years. Brand transformation is a strategic undertaking, not a quick fix. Great brands don't become great brands overnight.

Emotional Rescue

Seeking emotional connections takes you from differentiating your offering to profiting from long-term relationships to successfully extending into new categories, and ultimately to creating new businesses. That's why great brands avoid selling products.

When Scott Bedbury looks back on Nike's unveiling of the "Just Do It" campaign, he compares it to the unlocking of the brand's "genetic code." The tagline, he writes, "codified an ethos that had always existed within the Nike brand, that was part of its genetic structure long before [the agency] identified it." Nike, he says, just couldn't see it until "our backs were up against the wall and had to dig deeply into what made the brand tick."[20]

Digging deep for that genetic code has made all the difference for Nike. Like other great brands, it has used its brand essence as a source of inspiration for connecting emotionally with its customers and for moving its product line far beyond the running category that might have once confined it. The problem, though, is that this is not what most companies do when they have their backs to the wall. For many reasons that are very understandable, they look for quick fixes. They do market research to figure out what's hot. They stick their fingers in the wind, figuratively speaking, to see which way it's blowing. Rather than rely on their culture and their emotional connections with customers to inform their next moves, most brands do what great brands don't do: they try to follow trends.

CHAPTER 3

Great Brands Ignore Trends

When Oprah Winfrey ended her popular TV show in 2011, most of the media pointed out the many accomplishments Winfrey had achieved in becoming a billionaire media mogul—enlivening daytime talk programming, repopularizing reading and book buying through Oprah's Book Club, and winning an Academy Award nomination, just to name a few.

But media critic David Carr used the opportunity to point out in an essay that the Oprah brand was much more distinctive for what Winfrey chose *not* to do. Unlike many other talk show hosts, she took herself off the air when her show was still successful and one of the most effective branding platforms ever created. Unlike Martha Stewart and other media personalities, she never took her production holdings public or licensed out her name for use on products. Unlike so many other billionaire moguls, she never pursued bad business deals outside her area of core competence.

"If you are out to build a brand, you have to know what is real and right for you," Anna Wintour, editor of *Vogue*, told Carr. Arianna Huffington added, "She was transparent and authentic before those things were cool." And as brand strategist Jonathan

Salem Baskin put it, "Winfrey tapped into consumers' need for trusted personal referrals long before social media platforms like Facebook and Twitter capitalized on it."[1]

Oprah ignored nearly all the trends in her rarefied field and, as a result, she created her own movement. Her strategy stands out as a singular achievement in part because it's so rare, which might suggest that ignoring trends or bucking them is too risky for those of us who aren't Oprah. But the truth is that ignoring trends is what great brands do.

This chapter explains why trend-following is actually the more risky approach, and then describes two superior strategies: challenging trends, and anticipating and advancing cultural movements. It turns out that taking a counterintuitive approach to trends connects and elevates the first two brand-building principles in this book, "Great Brands Start Inside" and "Great Brands Avoid Selling Products." Great brands connect their internal culture to larger culture movements to establish authentic relevance and deeper emotional connections.

The Risky Business of Trend Following

We all know how strong the temptation is to go along with the crowd. If everyone's doing it, how wrong can it be? Besides, who wants to expose their company to getting left behind, to being excluded from the Next Big Thing? Trend following makes sense for lots of reasons, including the fact that it often is the simplest and most direct way for any business to raise short-term revenue.

Tapping into hot categories and riding the wave of fashionable trends are how brand managers can be assured that their brands will be noticed and talked about. Reebok, for instance, used the aerobics dance trend in the early 1980s for its well-timed introduction of the first exercise shoe designed for women.

The hit status of that product led to Reebok's $68 million IPO, one of the most successful public offerings made in 1985.[2]

Examples such as Reebok can make trend following seem like a smart strategy, but following someone else's lead usually results in what I call the "-er positioning" problem. To the consumer's mind, your products are just like another brand's products, but yours are small-er, bigg-er, thinn-er, light-er, fast-er, sexi-er, or simply just bett-er. Hyundai is an -er brand: "We're just as good as Lexus but cheap-er." Burger King is an -er brand, copying McDonald's smoothies and wraps with claims to be light-er and healthi-er. Even Walmart plays the -er role to great brand Target, with its constant emphasis on low-er prices.

An -er position is a dangerous place to be. Not only does it relegate your brand to subordinate status compared to the brand used as your reference point, it also tells customers that your brand possesses only comparative value, rather than having its own inherent value. Your value proposition becomes "just as good as Brand X, but _____-er." Do that and your brand will soon be under constant pressure to introduce another new product on Brand X's time line, because now your brand value is tied to Brand X's product. You become only as good as your next product, which is absolutely not what great brands do.

Great brands also don't try to be the arbiter of coolness. And yet, each year, we see this endeavor during the Christmas shopping season, when all the nation's top retailers vie to be the first to publish the "hot list" of toys for the season, even though all they're doing is diminishing their role and value as a brand. Instead of doing things that highlight the uniqueness of their brand and customer experience and help develop long-term relationships with customers, they're positioning themselves as simply the channel through which customers buy the popular products this season. The brand equity they try to borrow from the hot products' coolness isn't ownable. And it's not sustainable—the products may be hot today, but they're unlikely to be popular next year, and so retailers wind up in a never-ending chase after what's hot. I'm still waiting to see the first retailer break from the pack on this practice, but it seems that none want to take the risk of missing out.

Many companies prefer trend following to true innovation because it seems so much safer and easier to interpret someone else's proven product than to bank on your own original-but-untested idea. The main trouble with this thinking is that just because something is working for one brand doesn't mean it will work for yours. The context and execution of a strategy will always have a greater impact on your results than your choice of which trend or style to chase after.

Trend following in general isn't quite as safe as most people think, especially since trends come and go more quickly than ever these days. Products, ideas, themes, and personalities become popular overnight, saturate the collective consciousness, and then drop from fashion as quickly as they appeared. Such a rapid life cycle wreaks havoc on efforts to build a sustainable brand image, not to mention planning and managing inventory.

Teenage apparel retailers such as Hot Topic, American Eagle Outfitters, and Pacific Sun illustrate the difficulties of trend following—the financial performance of each company has been on a roller-coaster ride for several years. For example, when Hot Topic opened its first store in 1987, its edgy styles were a hit among teens bored with preppy Tommy Hilfiger and similar conservative brands. But then as the punk look faded from popularity in the early 90s, so did Hot Topic's performance. Now the chain seems back on an upswing thanks to the cultural currency of vampire themes in teenage movies and books, but how long will that last?

Inevitably, the practice of following trends lures companies into betraying the first two principles of brand as business. Trend following almost always leads companies to create products and services that are inconsistent with their internal culture. And, even at its best, trend following forces ways of thinking and strategizing that revolve around products, features, and benefits, which is exactly what great brands don't do.

At its worst, trend following encourages a culture of novelty seeking, which kills off true innovation. Then the ultimate risk is that if you're seeking inspiration by drawing on the same narrow range of information as everyone else, you're going to end up with products and solutions that everyone else already has. The fact that everyone is doing something is exactly why your results will be limited. You have no chance to stand out. Your sameness tests your fans' abilities to see you as being a distinctive brand that they should make a deliberate choice to engage with.

Instead, great brands challenge trends.

Challenging Business-as-Usual

In 1991, Steve Ells couldn't afford to eat regularly at the legendary Stars restaurant where he was working as a $12-an-hour line cook. Instead, he was more frequently found gorging himself on giant burritos at a taquería in San Francisco's Mission District called Zona Rosa. It was there, over a carnitas burrito, that Ells had the insight that would change his life—and American fast food—forever.

Ells looked up from his table at the long line of people waiting to order their food and the small group of workers behind the counter preparing the rice, beans, pork, and guacamole. "I remember jotting down on a napkin at that moment how many people were going through the line, how quickly," he told the *Rocky Mountain News* in 2006, "and I thought, they probably have this much in sales, the food costs might be X—a good little business."[3]

As a trained chef and graduate of the Culinary Institute of America, Ells was intrigued by something else about Zona Rosa. Its food was produced fast and inexpensively, but the quality and the flavor weren't compromised in the way that typical fast food fare is. He returned to his hometown—Boulder, Colorado—and there in 1993 he opened the first in a chain of Chipotle Mexican Grills.[4]

There are now more than 1,400 Chipotle locations in forty-three states, and the chain reportedly made a 25 percent profit margin on $2 billion in sales in 2011.[5]

Chipotle began a trend in restaurants that the industry has dubbed "fast casual," which offers a more upscale dining environment and food quality, along with higher prices, but in the familiar, convenient limited service format of fast food. "When I started Chipotle, I didn't know the fast-food rules," Ells explained years later. "People told us the food was too expensive and the menu was too limited. Neither turned out to be true."[6]

By either ignoring or directly challenging all the dominant trends in its industry, Chipotle quickly became a great brand. Now Chipotle has become the trendsetter in the category, and trade publications feature headlines such as "Who Will Be the Chipotle of Pizza?"[7] Wendy's and Taco Bell are just two of the most prominent fast food players investing in new store designs that look shockingly similar to that of Chipotle. The *Wall Street Journal* dubbed Ells the "Fast Food Revolutionary," and *Esquire* crowned him America's most admired CEO.[8]

A Challenger Brand That Challenges Everything

The common wisdom in the fast food industry has always been that you grind out your profits through reduced prices, expanded menus, and efficient operations. At the time of Chipotle's founding, Taco Bell—the putative head-on competitor to Chipotle in the Mexican food category—was turning heads in the industry with its enormously successful penny-pinching "59–79–99" value menu.

But Ells grew Chipotle by going in the opposite direction. He determined that Chipotle could introduce a higher quality of Mexican fare to a broader audience by defining a different value equation for fast food. All the food would be freshly prepared. The ingredients would be top quality. And the restaurants themselves would be beautiful, all wood and metal, offering a dining experience several notches above fast-food Formica counters and fluorescent lighting.

Efficiencies in the fast food industry depend largely upon limiting spoilage and minimizing labor costs by cooking frozen meat patties and French fries, but Chipotle restaurants don't even have freezers. All of Chipotle's ingredients are delivered fresh. After the company bought hundreds of labor-saving onion-slicing machines, Ells ordered that onions go back to being hand-cut because he felt that that made them taste better. Machine cutting had left the onions a little dried out.[9]

Another standard fast-food practice is to pay employees as little as possible. By contrast, Chipotle's practice is to pay more, but to dismiss employees who lack energy or are otherwise mediocre performers. (One industry observer marveled, "Who ever heard of a fast-food restaurant firing someone for being mediocre?")[10]

Despite its higher wages, however, Chipotle still manages to spend more on ingredients than it does on payroll, the exact reverse of the fast food formula for success. In the years when other restaurants of all kinds were cutting prices in a race to bottom, Chipotle either held fast or raised prices. For instance, when Ells was unhappy with the taste of his shredded pork burrito, he went out and sourced a higher grade of pork and raised the burrito's price by a dollar, and sales of the product reportedly doubled to a full 8 percent of company revenue.[11]

In the course of Chipotle's rise from one store to more than 1,400, the company has faced countless temptations to stray from its distinct course and lapse into following trends. Much of Chipotle's early growth had been financed by a large investment from McDonald's Corporation, and executives there failed in their efforts to get Chipotle to offer low-risk high-profit menu items such as cookies and coffee. "They probably did give me grief," Ells modestly explained to *Time* magazine in 2012. "We wouldn't do [cookies and coffee] better than anyone else. And I don't want anything to be part of Chipotle that wouldn't be the very best."

McDonald's sold its stake in Chipotle in 2006, and since then, Chipotle has moved further and further away from the typical fast food way of doing business. Ells's latest obsession is the issue of sustainability. Chipotle is now the largest buyer of higher-priced pork, beef, and chicken from animals that have been naturally fed and humanely raised outside the factory-farming system, which provides inexpensive commodity meats to the rest of the food industry.[12] Produce served at Chipotle is also locally raised if possible (lettuce served in January on the East Coast still comes from California).[13] What Chipotle has learned is that customers notice the difference in flavor from natural meats and fresh vegetables grown "with integrity," as the chain's tagline states—and they're willing to pay extra for it.

Challenging Conventions

Resisting the urge to compete on price is a difficult path that people in all industries face. It's a particularly critical decision among premium and luxury brands. Tiffany & Co., for instance, addressed falling revenues during the 2008–2009 recession by quietly cutting prices on engagement rings by 10 percent. Customers were informed of the reductions by salespeople in the stores, but there was no advertising of a "sale" of any kind, for fear of damaging the Tiffany brand.

Saks Fifth Avenue and other luxury retailers, by contrast, followed the price-cutting trend. They held big sales announcing as much as 70 percent off, and claimed they managed to do it without diminishing their brand images. But the executives at Tiffany & Co. saw it the other way, and bucked the trend at great short-term cost. "It's about maintaining the long-term value of the enterprise," Tiffany & Co.'s CEO Michael Kowalski said in 2009. "If we were to abandon that, the consequences would be significant."[14] Despite the company's decision to hold firm on pricing, it has produced an annualized double-digit growth rate over the last decade and remains supported by analysts and investors who have "extreme confidence in Tiffany's long-term story."[15]

Not only can challenging trends prove to be more profitable, it can also open areas of greater business scope and impact. Around 2008, the fantastically successful annual TED conference in Long Beach, California, was coming under fire for its exclusive, elitist format, in which limited numbers of people are invited to attend at ticket prices starting at $6,000. What had been conceived as an effort to discover and discuss "ideas worth spreading" was in danger of looking like a country club for elitist thinkers.[16]

Pressure from the outside first induced TED executives to put videos of TED talks on its website for free access to the public. That led to an even more radical idea: to have mini-TED conferences, called TEDx, all over the world, run by volunteer groups who apply for a license from the TED organization but otherwise operate independently. Going in this direction was cutting against some major received wisdom in the business world. Said Bruno Giussani, TEDGlobal director at the time, "One of the mantras of management for the past 20 years has been that you must be obsessive about protecting your brand."[17] TED leaders decided to go the other way, giving the brand away for free, with only the most tenuous strings attached.

TED owner and leader Chris Anderson acknowledged the risk involved, and told the *New York Times* that he was facing questions of "How do you avoid damaging the TED brand? Can you package TED in a box?"[18] Three years later, after more than 5,700 TEDx conferences held in more than 130 countries, the doubts have been silenced definitively by TED's widespread popularity and influence.

Now Anderson and others at TED are looking into the possibility that TED talk videos can contribute to education systems around the world. This is the kind of new growth opportunities that you can expect when you scorn prevailing wisdom and challenge trends. Moreover, as TED has become the model of a new kind of organization that relies on fans of the brand to help it grow and develop, it shows how great brands actually create their own trends.

Anticipating and Advancing Cultural Movements

The managers of great brands don't operate in a reactive mode, waiting to jump on the next bandwagon. They take note of bandwagons, and then, without jumping aboard, question what all those bandwagons might suggest about the future. They identify powerful ideas on the horizon and discover ways to advance them, which is very different from following trends.

That's the secret to growth. You take a proactive approach to anticipating cultural movements, instead of a reactive approach to chasing transitory trends. The proactive approach can spell the difference between leadership—where the growth is—and mere followership as just another member of a crowded field of -er brands.

The difference between a trend and a movement might be difficult to grasp at times, and it is true that often the toughest choices of this kind are made by courageous and self-assured leaders like Oprah Winfrey and Steve Ells. One of the dangers I see in recounting such CEO-as-hero stories is that they carry an underlying message that only special leaders with natural gut instincts can defy the trends that others must follow.

The truth is that, although your instincts are valuable, there are reasonable and rational ways of assessing the risks and rewards in choosing whether to try and lead a movement or merely to follow a trend. It takes foresight, dedication, and a good bit of courage—and there's always a chance you'll misread the cultural currents and wind up left out of the game, as so many trend-following brands fear. I think it's instructive that, while Oprah always seems to be taking great risks with her brand, she also seems to have an awareness that there are no sure things in life. Just in case something goes wrong, she is said to keep $50 million of her investments in cash alone for something she calls her "bag lady fund" to be used if her fortune changes.[19]

Even with a safety net, leading companies don't leave these important matters to chance, whim, or the CEO's gut. They constantly scan the cultural environment for signs of meaningful, long-lasting change that might affect them. They keep abreast of technology, demographics, consumer tastes, laws, resource prices, and competitive behavior, and then they identify possible ways to exploit movements in these fields. They do this because they know that growth comes from being proactive—anticipating or leading change.

Starbucks and Lady Gaga Lead Change

If you try to tap into something that's already happening, you're likely to get caught chasing a trend like everyone else. Instead, you want to try to connect with the larger culture in terms that are relevant to your brand and what it stands for. The opportunity is to decipher where society is going in the long term and analyze how your brand can add value in ways that are consistent with that direction, while staying true to your culture and your existing emotional connections with your customers.

Starbucks, for instance, has been about more than coffee from its inception. The brand gained traction in its early years by designing shops as anchors of community life, as a "third place" outside home and work. CEO Howard Schultz saw an opportunity to respond to the phenomenon of increasing isolation in American society by introducing Italian coffeehouse culture and the casual social interaction it fosters.

Now, with the extraordinary advancements in mobile technology of late, the idea of place-based experiences is giving way to opportunities to connect with people wherever, whenever, and however they like. The company sees the potential of digital tools to build even more integral relationships with customers and is designing its business to be more fluid and open. It appointed its first-ever chief digital officer to pioneer developments in this emerging space that other businesses will be sure to copy in the future.[20]

Just as Starbucks continues to transform the experience of coffee in modern life, Lady Gaga is transforming what it means to be a recording artist. Her album *ARTPOP* was released as a paid-for mobile phone app, launched "with chats, films for every song, extra music, Gaga-inspired games, fashion updates, magazines and more."[21] The reason is that Lady Gaga is at the forefront of the movement in personal celebrity engagement, which has arisen at the intersection of new communications technology and the democratization of the music and film industries.

Lady Gaga was one of the first to reach one billion views on her YouTube channel, and she's consistently one of the most-followed Twitter users, with more than 34 million signed up to get her tweets in 2013.[22] She continues to send out tweets on her own, and she guards against having anything promotional on her account, because that would break the trust she has with her millions of followers. The *ARTPOP* app takes Lady Gaga's engagement with her fans to a whole new level and advances a new movement in music culture.

Breaking from the Pack

Cultural movements seem obvious once they've taken hold, but anticipating them requires keen insight and courage. There is a magical moment in the movie *Soul Surfer* when the heroine, played by actress AnnaSophia Robb, makes a crucial choice. Robb plays the role of Bethany Hamilton, a twenty-four-year-old California woman who returned to competitive surfing after losing her right arm in a shark attack.

In the climactic competition of her comeback, she remained several points behind the leader with the clock running out. The film depicts the surfers all in a small circle in the ocean as they wait for the next wave to appear, but the water is calm.

Bethany is determined to win the competition, so she starts to paddle farther out, to an area far from the cluster of competitors. It's not obvious at first, but she sees something the others don't. With seconds to spare, a huge wave rises under Bethany and takes her on her best ride of the day. And because she had swum out to a spot where no one else was, she had the wave all to herself, securing her place in surfing history.

The next time you have to make a choice between bucking a trend or competing on the same basis as everyone else, try to think about Bethany Hamilton—all alone, paddling with her one remaining arm, heading out into the loneliness and danger of open water. Great brands make that swim. They move away from the crowd and explore new territory because that's a way to create greater opportunities for growth. Instead of looking where everyone else is looking and remaining in known territory, they scan the horizon and move in unexpected directions. Real growth happens when you catch a rising wave and no one else is nearby to share it with. Then you're riding a wave you can call your own.

This concept is very similar to the ideas advanced in the seminal best-selling book *Blue Ocean Strategy* by W. Chan Kim and Renée Mauborgne. Kim and Mauborgne's research into 150 significant strategic corporate moves (spanning more than thirty industries over a decade) revealed that companies grow best when they leave existing market spaces that are bloody with cut-throat competition (red oceans) and create instead uncontested market spaces (blue oceans). Specifically, the two discovered that of all 150 strategies, the 14 percent of those that managed to create blue oceans gained 38 percent of the revenues and 61 percent of the profits. Those companies achieved those results through a process the authors call "value innovation," which renders rivals obsolete and unleashes streams of new demand.[23]

A good example of a blue ocean strategy is that of Cirque du Soleil, which managed to redefine circus acts as theater, and in doing so, was able to charge the higher ticket prices that adults were used to paying for a theater show. Cirque responded to what Richard Rumelt, a UCLA business professor, calls a preexisting set of "value denials" among consumers. These are defined as "products or services that are both desired and feasible, but are not being supplied to the market."[24] In the case of Cirque du Soleil, circus acts are normally presented in cheesy "family-friendly" venues, with a lot of animals and hokey circus music. There had never been a place where adults and children could enjoy the beauty and excitement created by world-class jugglers, tumblers, and acrobats presented as a theater-like show with high-quality lighting, music, and costumes.

That was the value denial. No one was really asking for anything like Cirque until Cirque came along to provide it. Cirque was a lot like Starbucks in that sense. Prior to the opening of the first Starbucks, no consumer survey would have shown evidence of popular demand for a $5 cup of coffee. This doesn't mean value denials can't be detected through research, however. You just have to know what you're looking for.

Looking to the Horizon

To identify powerful ideas on the horizon, you have a few strategies at your disposal:

- *Scanning*. Continuously monitor different media, cultural developments, and the activities of brands in and outside your category, and identify the meanings behind them. Look for new consumer attitudes and behaviors and try to discern how and why different groups and organizations engage with them. Maclaren, the baby stroller maker, took note of evolving parental roles, including a rising number of stay-at-home fathers and fathers in same-sex marriages, and men's growing influence on purchase categories traditionally assumed by women. These observations led the company to introduce a new stroller, the BMW Buggy, and promote it as sophisticated and high-performance.

- *Listening*. Use social networks to identify cultural influences. Listening has become a common marketing practice, but keep in mind it's not as important to know *what* is trending on Twitter, for example, as it is to understand *who* is prompting the discussion and *why*. The popularity of the "Gangnam Style" video that swept through the social networks in 2012 pointed to a more significant development—the growing Korean wave of influence on Western popular culture. The buzz generated by any one of First Lady Michelle Obama's clothing choices is less about the specific brand, designer, or style she selected and more about her role as a tastemaker. Topics come and go, sometimes in a day. Underlying values and the communities that influence topics tend to have a longer shelf life.

- *Forecasting*. Search the databases of trend-forecasting service firms like Cassandra Daily and PSFK. Look for common themes across new developments and keep an eye out for innovations in seemingly unrelated fields that might influence your customers. While many companies engage in some sort of trend monitoring, few examine developments outside their category and existing customer market. But some of the changes with most impact on your business may come from unexpected places. Had those in the rental car market been monitoring developments in mobile technology, they might have seen how their business model would be seriously disrupted by Uber and Zipcar.

Keeping a sustained relevance to consumers requires a much deeper interpretation and understanding of what's going on in society than the mere observation of what's hot. The goal is to understand the role of your brand in people's lives and in broader culture and then anticipate how that role can, will, or should change. You don't want to jump on obvious bandwagons. Instead, you want to practice pattern recognition from among a number of different sources, determining what they all mean taken together.

◆ Tool: Performing a Brand Diagnostic

If your company is using scanning, listening, and forecasting to explore uncharted territory, you can initiate a "Brand Diagnostic" process to assess your brand's current strengths, identify opportunities to grow the brand in those new areas, and map the unconventional methods to carry them out.

A Brand Diagnostic is derived from the brand-as-business mentality—it puts all areas of the business, not only marketing efforts, under investigation; and it requires the CEO or COO to champion the process, not relegating it to a marketing-driven task. The best Brand Diagnostics are conducted by cross-functional teams working together with outsiders who can offer perspectives to ensure the assessment is objective. If you can't do that, or if you want to make progress in the meantime while summoning the budget for that kind of effort, there are still some steps you can take to inform your decision making so that you're not falling into the trap of copying products, cutting prices, and following trends.

A Brand Diagnostic looks at your brand through three critical lenses:

- *Customers:* Determine what the demand landscape of your category looks like. What are people's needs, wants, usage occasions, and drivers of purchase and repurchase? How well are you meeting these needs and speaking to these drivers? How are customers' lives and their needs and wants changing? What changes will generate new purchase and usage drivers? Who are the brand's target segments? What do they think of your brand? What value should you deliver to them in order to meet their needs and wants? How solid are your customer relationships? Are you being actively chosen and preferred, or is your business susceptible to customer defection?

- *Context:* Consider both the competitive context and the broader context. Who are the company's key competitors today? Why do people choose them over you and vice versa? How will the competitive landscape change? What are your brand's strengths and vulnerabilities? Are you well-positioned to compete and grow as it changes? What new opportunities will open up in the marketplace that you should prepare for? What category trends and macro factors (including the economy, technological developments, political factors, cultural influences, and social trends) will affect the company's business in the next five to ten years?

- *Company:* Examine your organization and your brand strategy. How well are you fulfilling your purpose and operationalizing your values? What factors have been driving your performance? Which strategies and tactics are working and which aren't? How will your organization have to evolve or change to meet your goals? What assets, core competencies, and centers of excellence do you have that could be better employed to grow the business? What is your current brand strategy? Is your brand healthy and strong? How do you establish and sustain relevant and energized differentiation? Look at all your products and services, including those in the pipeline, and review how they are sold and distributed and how they are currently positioned.

The Brand Diagnostic is a thorough analysis that involves the following action steps:

1. *Desk research and industry data mining.* This is the fundamental fact finding, which mostly deals with identifying category trends and macro factors through analysis of syndicated data, analysts' reports, and market overviews.

2. *Analysis of existing consumer research.* This primarily helps answer the questions of the customer lens. If your company doesn't have research data that shows, for example, what drives purchases in the category and for specific brands, you need to conduct primary market research to get the answers.

3. *In-depth interviews with key stakeholders including executives, frontline employees, investors, partners, customers, and distributors.* These are wide-ranging interviews usually conducted by an outside expert, somewhat akin to the kind of assessment a personal trainer might give a new client. A trainer starts with the client's goals and then performs routine tests and measurements to assess the client's fitness and ability to reach those goals. Only then can the trainer determine the steps and changes necessary to reach the desired goal. The overall objective of internal interviews is to understand the key business and brand issues that are impacting the company and to suss out individual perceptions and beliefs regarding the current strengths of and challenges to the brand relative to the growth goals. Interviews with external stakeholders provide a reality check against internal perceptions, which can be distorted by habit, pet projects, and internal politics.

4. *Investigative audit of the brand experiences and communication for your brand and key competitors.* This means taking the simple steps of shopping for and buying the product, opening the packaging, using the product, contacting customer service, joining the loyalty program, returning the product, and engaging in every other form of contact a customer is likely to have with your brand. It also entails collecting all advertising, promotions, Internet and social media programs, PR, and corporate communications. You want to do this for your brand and key current and emerging competitors, investigating each on the four P's—product, price, place, and promotion—and identifying the category conventions in all four areas. For example, if most competitors use broadcast media, that may reveal the opportunity to differentiate your brand by using print, social, or outdoor media.

From this information, you can determine how different companies are positioning their brands, what they are choosing to prioritize, how big the gap is between brand communication and brand experience—between what a brand says about itself and what the company actually does—and other insights about how the different brands in your competitive landscape shape up.

Understanding what you're really up against may also necessitate looking at your brand through the prism of how you compare with players in categories far afield from your traditionally defined competition. As Coca-Cola's Jonathan Mildenhall puts it, "We have two sets of competition, category competition and competition within the space of the purpose we're trying to communicate. In terms of understanding where popular culture is going, we're going to be much more successful if we look at businesses and brands in the space of happiness than if we just look at the beverage category."[25]

5. *Investigative channel audit.* You never know what you're going to find when you take the time to enter a store and look at the displays, make notes of actual product placements, and

interact with salespeople. Many managers whose brands are sold through online stores never bother to use search engines and comparison sites to see how the brand appears to the outside world in those channels. And how can you be sure how well your e-commerce strategy represents your brand if you never try shopping for a product, using the filtering functionality, researching product details, and checking out with your purchase?

For one packaged goods client, I took pictures of the product category on the shelves of grocery stores. When the executives were confronted with images of the ten feet of shelf space for the category and how their product was barely noticeable among all the others, we talked about the importance of standing out in that environment and we put redesigning the packaging and negotiating better placements on the list of possible priorities. In these and many other cases, you might find it takes the deliberate and objective eye of an outsider to point out elements of the shopping experience to help people see what's right in front of them.

It's Not the Data; It's What You Do with It

I realize all these steps might sound elementary, and they may be routine for you. Applying this approach may not require a change in the data you collect, but it's likely to call for a change in what you do with it. I've found that most companies involved in the day-to-day hustle for quarterly results can lose track of the aggregate data and knowledge at their command. In that case, it can be very helpful to simply collect and analyze all existing data and then use that to paint a cohesive picture of the state of the brand. One client had spent over $1 million a year in research for each of the five years leading up to my work with it. But its people had never really analyzed the data in a way that made a difference in operations or helped them make substantive changes. Only after I pulled out the key data from several studies, put them all on one poster, and asked the executive team to draw their own conclusions did they actually come to grips with how poorly they were executing in certain areas.

All this insight and information goes into an objective-based SWOT analysis—looking at your brand strengths, weaknesses, opportunities, and threats relative to your business objective. Your objective might be to extend into new categories or geographies, or to increase your price premium, or to attract a new customer segment. The objective-based SWOT analysis, in turn, leads to an evaluation of your brand on criteria including differentiation (is your brand distinctly different from competitive offerings? do your target customers perceive the difference and think it's important?), transcendence (does your brand convey value beyond a specific product, per Chapter Two?), and experiential consistency (is your brand expressed and delivered consistently across all touchpoints—not just in advertising and marketing communications, but across every point between the company and the outside world?).

The Brand Diagnostic is a tool for taking stock of both assets and liabilities in terms of brand equity that your company probably didn't know it had. In one such diagnostic for a national specialty retailer, we concluded that its broad assortment of products (a source of pride for the company) was actually limiting sales and revenues. The assortment had gotten so unfocused that consumers had trouble navigating all the choices before them and were getting confused about what the brand really stood for. We developed a growth plan that involved streamlining the categories the retailer sold and tightly editing the selection within each category.

Such steps are highly counterintuitive, since more variety usually means more revenue, but great brands offer many examples of how a limited selection of offerings sharpens the brand image and appeal. Apple CEO Tim Cook has observed that he could display all of Apple's products all at once on his desk, and he said it as a testament to his company's focus and self-confidence in its brand identity.

With the retailer I just mentioned, we also discovered that sales of different products varied greatly with channels of trade. The brand's electronic gadgets and luxury items sold best in upscale suburban malls, while health and wellness items sold better in lifestyle centers. Another category, travel-related products, sold best in high-tourism areas like New York City. We recommended that the retailer consider changing from a national assortment strategy to one in which local stores would focus on specific categories and product lines best suited to them.

The retailer ultimately decided this step wouldn't be worth the trouble—too many headaches involved in managing inventory and devising multiple promotional strategies, employee training programs, and other activities. They also had a legitimate concern from a brand consistency standpoint. They wondered if they would disappoint or confuse customers who expected to find the same assortment of goods at every store.

I mention this example to emphasize that the purpose of the diagnostic is to bring *possibilities* to the surface for consideration. A Brand Diagnostic doesn't produce a plan of what must be done. In this case, removing certain items from stores where they are unpopular would run the risk of breaking the emotional connection with some customers. The potential savings weren't worth that risk.

A Brand Diagnostic I conducted for a women's accessories brand revealed that its existing position was causing it to miss out on a wide range of emerging opportunities. Historically, it had been positioned as a high-end niche brand, targeted to style-conscious women for use on specific occasions and sold at finer department stores. Because the brand had been the pioneer in this market, it had resonated with consumers and grown very quickly. But the customer and internal interviews and the competitive analysis I conducted in the Brand Diagnostic evaluation revealed that over time copycat competitors had reduced the brand's perceived uniqueness. Growth stalled as a result.

The market analysis and channel investigation I conducted helped the company see how future growth potential through department stores was limited because department stores weren't growing as a channel. At the same time my cultural scanning and channel trends analysis identified new channel innovations such as mobile shopping, temporary locations (pop-up shops), vending machines, and subscription services.

At the time, no other brand in the accessories space was using any of these innovations, suggesting that these channels were all potential areas of great opportunity. The investigation of company capabilities and assets also revealed how the company could produce different packaging and point-of-purchase materials that would make it easier for the product to sell itself through self-purchase channels like vending machines and high-volume pop-up locations. Further, my client and I identified the company's customer database as an underutilized asset—the company had only been using it for e-mail marketing programs, whereas the direct customer contact and the purchase data that had been collected could be used to initiate a subscription-based service. We concluded that pioneering these opportunities would reestablish the perceived differentiation the company had lost, enable it to reach new customers, and position the brand as a trendsetter in the category.

How you interpret what you see is critical to identifying the right trajectory. How many frozen yogurt places were opened and then rapidly shuttered after the success of Pinkberry and Red Mango led people to believe that they represented a movement and not a trend? What if Steve Ells, sitting in that taquería, had interpreted his insight about the "nice little business" to mean that Mexican food would be a big thing and positioned the Chipotle brand based on that? Instead, Chipotle grew up by attending to much bigger and more powerful movements, such as "affordable luxuries," "sustainable and natural food," and "health and wellness," all of which favor and inform the development of the Chipotle brand. The sustainable food movement now, in particular, is not just appealing to consumers' existing sensibilities about sustainable ingredients, it is also advancing people's understanding of its many benefits.

Achieving this kind of relevance is a result of anticipating and advancing cultural movements. Sustaining relevance involves more than just an external orientation. Great brands actually connect their internal brand culture to larger cultural movements to establish authentic relevance and deeper emotional connections.

Making the Internal Connection

In 2006, Steve Ells and his team at Chipotle became more thoughtful about their food sources at precisely the same time that sustainable food entered American's collective conscience. At that point, Chipotle became more than a business—it became a force of change. It became part of a movement.

Movements represent forces that shape the way people interact with others and with brands. Movements are also ways people interact with the companies they work for and the jobs they do. Lululemon Athletica employees are part of the movement that's making yoga more than just an exercise routine. Zappos employees are on a mission to "wow" customers. There's a "make flying fun" movement going on among Southwest Airlines employees. Strong internal cultures naturally give birth to internal movements, and when internal and external movements intersect, the impact on your business is exponential.

Integrating the internal and external comes from connecting and elevating the first two brand-building principles in this book: Start Inside and Avoid Selling Products. The goal is to understand the role of your brand in people's lives and in broader culture and then anticipate how it's likely to change and how you want it to change. The more clearly you can see your brand's external cultural relevance, the better you are able to align it with your internal culture and with the emotional connection to your customers—and vice versa. Lululemon, Zappos, Southwest, and other great brands advance cultural movements that resonate inside their organizations and out.

The connection between external and internal culture is so strong for Zumba Fitness that the line between the two worlds has become blurred. The fitness dance program that started in a single gym in Florida became an international mass-market phenomenon in less than ten years by being at the forefront of what one *Inc.* magazine writer describes as "a frothy blend" of cultural movements including "Latin culture, social networking, globalization, weight consciousness, a feminizing society, solo entrepreneurship, and the maker's movement." The essence of Zumba culture—"FEJ" (pronounced "fedge" and standing for Freeing, Electrifying Joy)—has sparked a powerful movement that touches 14 million people every week. FEJ is cultivated both internally and externally as the company releases a constant stream of videos, conferences, apparel, equipment, and music conceived by its free-spirited and charismatic founders, while many students become trained as instructors and then equipped as entrepreneurs who run their own Zumba communities and evangelists who recruit new students and instructors. This self-reinforcing loop of cultural relevance has produced remarkable results on critical dimensions: CEO Alberto Perlman says the company grew 4,000 percent from 2007 to 2010 and 750 percent from 2010 to 2012; *Billboard* has hailed Zumba as the next major music platform because of the volume of music distribution, commission, and production it is responsible for; and *Inc.* noted the healthy, flexible, and strong business model behind Zumba and named it 2012 Company of the Year.[26]

Ultimately pursuing these new cultural opportunities is a question of capabilities. Not only operational capabilities—whether or not you can build on existing organizational competencies, evolve the business strategy, and continue to support the new category through innovation—but also (and perhaps more important) brand capabilities. You need to be able to expand your strategic position while staying true to the essence of your brand. There is some danger in allowing the allure of a cultural movement to tempt you to chase too many opportunities and risk diluting your brand meaning and diffusing its focus. You must be able to develop a sustainable position by actively managing customers' perceptions of the new offering and asserting a dominant brand position from the start. Also you need to be able to modify, reposition, or rebrand your existing offerings to support the new ones.

Brands that succeed in rethinking their businesses along these lines can enjoy significant rewards. Ed Lebar and John Gerzema, authors of *The Brand Bubble*, call such brands "energized brands," which they define as "market leaders that set new expectations for the way things should be. They don't aim for mere awareness. Instead, they upend ideologies, challenge convention, and market themselves to consumers' value systems. They tap into mind-sets that find business in a broader cross-section of the marketplace, attracting new users and growing their categories."[27]

Lebar and Gerzema's list of energized brands wouldn't surprise many people. It includes great brands such as Target, Nike, GE, Toyota, and Apple. Great brands such as these create trends for others to follow. Often they discover a small group of people headed in a compelling direction, they use their resources to get out in front, and end up leading a full-blown parade.

Create Your Own Future

Every company chooses whether it wants to be a great brand or an -er brand. Every brand has a choice. Great brands ignore trends because they are unwilling to surrender their company culture and emotional connections with customers to the whims of the marketplace. Ultimately, by challenging trends and starting movements of their own, great brands give their customers more opportunities to engage with them. By connecting internal culture to broader cultural movements, great brands create futures in which they thrive and grow.

If there is one thing that Oprah, Chipotle, Starbucks, Lady Gaga, and many other great brands have in common, it is that they all have their share of detractors, almost as though that were a necessary by-product of going against the grain. Great brands don't mind detractors too much for the same reason they ignore trends. Great brands know that if you try to be all things to all people, you'll never connect deeply with anyone.

CHAPTER 4

Great Brands Don't Chase Customers

Lululemon Athletica has become one of the fastest-growing retailers in the world by doing a lot of nice things for its customers. The highly trained Lululemon staff members, called "educators," offer plenty of personal attention and advice to customers, whom they refer to as their "guests." Lululemon hosts free yoga classes and running clubs at its locations, even for the benefit of "guests" who never buy anything. In every way it can, Lululemon tries to build a sense of community around each of its retail stores.

But one decidedly unfriendly feature at Lululemon is its strictly enforced return policy. The goods must be brought back unwashed and unworn, with original tags still attached, and nothing is accepted more than fourteen days after purchase. "We aren't Nordstrom," Lululemon's former CEO Christine Day told the *Wall Street Journal*.[1]

Lululemon products are also priced a good deal higher than those of its competitors, and its core items are never discounted on sale. "If you want the cheapest product out there," explains Laura Klauberg, Lululemon's senior vice president for brand and community, "there are plenty of places where you can find what you're looking for. But you'd be hard-pressed to find the level of quality and innovation in fabrics and finishes that we offer. And there's a cost with doing that, so that's why our prices are what they are. We don't try to appeal to everybody."[2]

Lululemon does not chase customers. It attracts the customers it wants by staying true to what it stands for. "The stuff costs what it costs," says Sean O'Connor, a Seattle-based branding consultant and a Lululemon brand ambassador. "They shouldn't have to apologize for having beautiful stores with beautiful people."[3]

We are all drawn to people who express certainty about who they are. We respond naturally to their self-confidence, and our relationships with brands are no different. Brands with integrity and self-confidence not only attract loyal and high-quality customers, they attract the kind of employees, business partners, suppliers, and investors who also appreciate those attributes. Great brands make the most of this attraction. They deliver superior customer experiences—without trying too hard to please.

The managers of great brands actually actively segment the market and seek out only those whose natural brand affinity makes them ideal customers. Not only does this selectivity reinforce the brand identity, it also enables their organizations to develop products, services, and standards tailored to meet their most valuable customers' specific needs. Ultimately, the brand-as-business management approach comes into play, as great brands put their brand—not customers—at the center of their customer strategy. A brand-based business strategy enables companies to develop valuable relationships with the right kind of customers and produces clarity and conviction for everyone who works on the business.

This fully brand-centric approach to customers starts first with compelling, not chasing, customers.

Using Magnetic Appeal to Attract Customers

We all know the cautionary equation that if you try to be all things to all people, you risk becoming nothing to anyone. But when it comes to target marketing, many companies are prone to drift in this hazardous direction nonetheless. They grow excessively concerned about alienating certain seemingly high-value customer groups, so they hedge their bets by casting too wide a marketing net. As a result, they struggle to stay focused, set clear priorities, and stick to them. On other occasions, a firm might blanch at the first sign of softening in a target market, and then move quickly to compromise its original vision. Executives resort to an improvised strategy that might seem less risky, but in the process they grow that much closer to becoming nothing to anyone.

Lululemon has taken the opposite tack. It has enjoyed meteoric growth by shaping consumer expectations around its goals and then inviting like-minded "guests" to engage with Lululemon on its distinctive terms. "The model for retail used to be, come here and be cool if you buy our product. The model that Lululemon is trying to build is, you're pretty cool, we'll be your partner in being your best possible self. And that kind of turns retail on its head," says Christian Buss, a Credit-Suisse analyst who follows the company.[4]

Lululemon's aversion to putting products on sale is an extension of the company's brand identity. The objective is to condition customers to buy an item at full price when they see it, rather than wait for the next sale. "We are a luxury brand," Laura Klauberg says. "We make a certain amount of product and the newness is what our guest wants. Our guest doesn't want to be wearing what everyone else is wearing in yoga class, so we only make a certain amount of product. When you see something in the store, you should buy it, because it may not be there tomor-row."[5] This "scarcity model" of retail supply puts inventory management and brand cachet ahead of what might be a natural desire to be popular with as many customers as possible.

"We have huge demand for what people love, so why should we be selling at 60 percent off?" Klauberg asks. "Retail has trained consumers to look to get a discount, and to ask, 'Why should I ever pay full price?'" Lululemon customers are trained to grab it before it's gone, which is related to the store's strict policy on returns. Says Klauberg, "Our brand is about driving innovation on constant basis—that's why we're loved. Some guests come into our stores literally every day, asking 'What's new?' So we need to keep our product assortment fresh. . . . If we accepted returns like other retailers, that would prevent us from sticking with the model that has been the engine driving our success."

Lululemon's clarity of purpose translates into policies and practices that distinguish the customer experience at its stores, so it attracts shoppers whose values resonate with Lululemon's. And it allows Lululemon to dispense with costly market research. "We don't do segmentation," Klauberg explains. "We are driven by our core guest. Our focus is on creating the best product in the world that's both functional and beautiful. That's what our guest wants." Lululemon's garments are designed for a very spe-cific type of athletic person, she says, adding, "However, we know that despite the fact that we design with a very specific muse in mind, we appeal to a wide range of guests, from middle school girls who aspire to use Lululemon products to sixty-year-old women who do yoga every day. We offer aspiration to a big cross-section of people but we're laser-focused on who we're designing product for and communicating to."[6]

Lululemon also dispenses with marketing in the traditional sense. Instead, the company recruits local "brand ambassadors" from among the ranks of athletes, trainers, and yoga teachers to help generate interest among the uninitiated. As CNBC marveled in 2012, upon Lululemon's debut in London, "How is it possible that a retailer with the fourth-highest sales per square foot in retail . . . not to mention same-stores sales growth of 20 percent last year, does not precede an international launch with a splashy marketing campaign?

"The answer is because they don't have to."[7]

The Rolling Stones Versus the Beatles

Marketers have a tendency to dilute their messages because they don't want their brands to seem exclusionary. They try to stay away from media, locations, sponsorships, and any other signals that seem overtly discriminating. The problem they create for themselves is this: If it doesn't provide a clearly appealing message to a discrete target, a brand will lack distinctiveness. It will have no draw. On the other hand, a sharply focused and clearly targeted message and offering resonates with some customers, even if it turns others off. It attracts attention to the brand, like a lighthouse.

Adam Morgan introduced the marketing world to the concept of "lighthouse brands" in *Eating the Big Fish: How Challenger Brands Can Compete Against Brand Leaders*. Morgan writes, "Success as a Challenger comes through developing a very clear sense of who or what you are as a brand/business and why—and then projecting that identity intensely, consistently, and saliently to the point where, like a lighthouse, consumers notice you (and know where you stand) even if they're not looking for you."[8] That's what he calls a "lighthouse identity."

The lighthouse concept, attracting people *who aren't even looking for you*, resonates deeply with me because I've seen far too many good brands squander their precious equity in efforts to chase elusive audiences. When you embrace and celebrate who you are, you attract the people who are destined to be your most loyal customers. Consumers find enormous appeal in brands that insistently communicate their strongly forged identities. "Challengers do not seem to plot their path by the rest of the world," Morgan explains. "They are confident enough to invite the world to navigate by them. . . . They have a very clear sense, first and foremost, of who they are, not as a sense of their own external image, but as a sense of their own internal identity. . . . Everything else in the company flows from this—behavior, image, communication, culture."[9]

This lighthouse approach contrasts with the much more typical "spotlight" approach, one in which companies analyze category data to determine which customer segments are the most profitable and worthy of a spotlight. Brand managers put these segments under virtual magnifying glasses, dissecting every nuance about them while attempting to design products and services to fill their needs. All too often, the pursuit of spotlight customers pulls companies into areas outside their competencies and off their brand messages. Like a nerdy teenager pursuing the cheerleading captain, the company fails to appeal to its target and fails to meet its own expectations.

During the rise of the Beatles in the early sixties, rock and roll promoters signed up plenty of imitator bands that tried to appeal to the vast new market of teenagers that Beatlemania had revealed. All these bands had the same moptop haircuts and wholesome uniformed look as the Beatles, and almost all of them are now long forgotten.

Then there was the Rolling Stones. Their young manager-producer saw in Mick Jagger and Keith Richards a chance to present a "darker, bluesier and more boldly sexual side of rock and roll in a kind of ongoing counterpoint with the Beatles' sunnier, more pop-oriented vistas."[10] The Stones dressed like their audiences, and their hair was unkempt. They had an impertinent bad-boy appeal and songs like "(I Can't Get No) Satisfaction" spoke to teenage rebellion and alienation in a way that the Beatles didn't.

"I don't think I've ever met a 'sort of' Stones fan," branding columnist Jonathan Salem Baskin wrote in 2012 for *Forbes*. "People are either into them or they're not, and the former are not only serious but they're serious evangelists. . . . Have you been told about this marketing concept called *lifetime customer value*? I think the Stones have it."[11]

The Rolling Stones have outlasted the Beatles by more than four decades. Longevity might be regarded as evidence that the Rolling Stones had something the Beatles lacked: a brand vision. For more than forty years, the Stones have called themselves "The World's Greatest Rock and Roll Band."[12] Guided by what is, in effect, a simple mission statement, the Rolling Stones have always known who they are, even as times, fashions, and technologies have changed.

"Brands with vision embody a clear direction and point of view on the world," write brand consultants John Gerzema and Ed Lebar for *Strategy+Business*.[13] "They convey what they're on this planet to achieve. Some brands promise to change the way people think; others seek to shift expectations about the way things are done. Vision-driven brands see farther; they galvanize and inspire consumers to join in."

And to think that the Stones claim it's "only rock and roll"!

A Strong Brand Identity Attracts the Ideal Customer

The grocery store category is so heavily based in mass appeal that Trader Joe's stands out as a true lighthouse brand. Trader Joe's has found a lucrative niche in the $680 billion retail food industry by knowing its customers and maintaining a laser-like focus on predicting and meeting their ever-changing needs. This includes store site selection, which is based not only on the typical educational attainment demographics but also in zip code concentrations of food and cooking magazine subscriptions.[14]

Fortune magazine describes Trader Joe's this way: "It's an offbeat, fun discovery zone that elevates food shopping from a chore to a cultural experience." The store combines "low-cost, yuppie-friendly staples (cage-free eggs and organic blue agave sweetener) and exotic, affordable luxuries—Belgian butter waffle cookies or Thai lime-and-chili cashews—that you simply can't find anyplace else." It doesn't matter if sometimes the exotica is just window-dressing. Trader Joe's pita chips are reportedly produced by a Pepsico subsidiary and Trader's Joe's yogurts on the East Coast are provided by Danone.[15] The company's brand appeal sublimates details such as these.

Trader Joe's inspires its customers' love—on Trader Joe's terms. The stores are small and the product selection is very narrow. As *Fortune* describes it, Trader Joe's constricted product range helps keep prices low. With ten varieties of peanut butter, instead of the forty varieties found at a typical supermarket, Trader Joe's does more volume on each of the ten varieties, helping secure deeper discounts from suppliers.[16] You can't get all your weekly shopping done there, but that doesn't deter certain customers from visiting the store faithfully and waiting in cash register lines ten people long—or more, as the case can be during rush hour.

A study led by Pepperdine University professor Mark Mallinger attributes Trader Joe's appeal and distinctiveness to its culture, which "involves the customers in an ongoing sense of discovery and adventure." This explains why competitors experience difficulty in copying Trader Joe's. Other stores that are accustomed to competing by widening their variety of choices can't keep up with Trader Joe's ability to align its restricted product mix with its very specific target market. Mallinger writes,

"[T]here are no substitutes for the combination of attributes provided by the TJ culture and customer experience, because at TJ, customers become part of the culture rather than merely experiencing it."[17]

Preserving the culture at Trader Joe's means avoiding supermarket-style conveyor belts at the checkout counters. The company even held off for a long time on installing bar-code scanners for fear it would turn off loyal customers who appreciated Trader Joe's more personal, small-store feel. Underlying everything Trader Joe's does is the desire "to establish a personal relationship with the customer."[18]

You Can't Please Everyone All the Time

"Customer service" has become such a business-world mantra that the idea of customer-centricity is easy to misunderstand. A brand can incur real opportunity costs by attempting to provide across-the-board excellence in customer service. When you try to treat everyone well, you risk withholding exceptional treatment from your best, most loyal customers.

Plus, without a strong sense of self, a brand doesn't inspire respect. In *Can't Buy Me Like: How Authentic Customer Connections Drive Superior Results*, advertising industry veterans Bob Garfield and Doug Levy observe that "businesses that prostrate themselves before customers at the expense of their own core vision, to say nothing of their dignity, evince no respect and therefore engender none. . . . People who patronize you do not wish to be patronized themselves."[19]

The managers of great brands, by contrast, have the courage and commitment to maintain their appeal among and focus only on those they consider their ideal customers. By never holding sales, Lululemon keeps bargain-hunters out of its stores. Trader Joe's doesn't offer coupons or loyalty cards, so everyone gets through the checkout line quicker. For great brands, the customer is *not* always right—only the right customers are always right.

Another grocer adheres to this principle—Whole Foods Market. The recent Great Recession dealt a body blow to fast-growing Whole Foods. Co-CEO Walter Robb describes the experience as "a lot of humble pie."[20] Whole Foods had earned the unfortunate nickname of "Whole Paycheck" because of its high prices, and when the recession pinched those paychecks, a good number of Whole Foods customers took their business elsewhere.

But Whole Foods' management realized that the customers who stayed were special. They were loyal to the brand because they enjoyed the experience of shopping their stores and they appreciated the company's values. "That was very affirming," Robb says, explaining that the company realized it should focus on those customers. "So instead of chasing every customer out there, we started doing customer discussion groups. . . . We cut the growth in half overnight and said, 'All right, slow down. Let's make sure we're doing this better and more thoroughly and more thoughtfully.'"[21]

Through the Whole Foods example, it's easy to see that targeting is not merely a way to achieve marketing efficiency. Targeting is a way to shore up brand equity, identify strategic possibilities, and determine operational focus. Targeting can be a prime driver of profit margins.

And yet, the 2011 Prophet State of Marketing Study found that even though 50 percent of marketing executives considered their current strategies well-targeted, more than 75 percent of them do not believe they're executing those strategies effectively. "Building a brand has never been more challenging," the study authors note. "[E]xploding and fragmenting channels have made customer relationships a moving target."[22]

If that's the case, then it matters now more than ever which customer relationships you choose to target. Peter Fader, Wharton professor and author of *Customer Centricity: Focus on the Right Customers for Strategic Advantage*, draws a line of distinction between brands that offer superior service to everyone, such as Nordstrom's, and the practice of customer-centricity as a targeted endeavor. According to Fader, "Customer centricity says, 'Let's find who the most valuable customers are and let's do everything for them,' [by offering] super duper service and more than that. For the other customers, [it says] 'Eh, we're glad to have their business, but it's going to be more on our terms than theirs.'" In Fader's estimation, the opportunity costs are too great to do otherwise.[23]

Sorting Out Lovers and Haters

Red Bull is one of those brands that has had little trouble figuring out who's important and who's not. It has become the most popular energy drink in the world with a brand personality so strong that Red Bull drinkers don't even care that the product doesn't taste very good. *BusinessWeek* reported that during Red Bull's early years, a British market research firm ran taste tests that concluded, "No other new product has failed this convincingly." But Red Bull founder Dietrich Mateschitz countered, "Taste is of no importance whatsoever." Instead, his product was intended to improve physical performance and "emotional status."[24]

In introducing Red Bull as a new product, part of Mateschitz's marketing genius involved setting up a website that actually *helped* nurture rumors that the beverage contained harmful ingredients. In response to reports that speculated that Red Bull was a dangerous drug, he explained it was far more "dangerous" for his product to generate no interest. Mateschitz claimed it was just as important to him that high school teachers hated Red Bull as it was that their students loved it. The brand's polarizing nature was part of the company's strategy. He said the aspiration was to "make the brand interesting enough that people wanted to get their hands on it."[25]

Speaking at the Advertising Research Foundation's annual conference, Thomas Grabner, then CEO of Kastner & Partners, Red Bull's advertising agency, explained how they clearly defined the brand personality to the point of being polarizing. They knew they "could not create passion by appealing to all people equally. If you stand for something, some people will love you and some will hate you, but the ones that love you will buy your brand and be willing to pay a premium for it."[26]

The Red Bull product line is very simple, limited to three drink varieties in the United States. Red Bull doesn't do licensing deals or brand extensions under an umbrella brand. The company also stays away from event sponsorships, preferring instead to develop its own distinctive promotions, mainly in extreme sports, which includes fielding its own Formula 1 racing team.[27] In 2012 Felix Baumgartner's world-record-breaking twenty-four-mile skydiving free fall was made from the Red Bull Stratos helium balloon and watched live by a record 8 million people on Red Bull's YouTube channel.[28] The Red Bull homepage is so crowded with daredevil sports videos and Red Bull music events listings, that it's easy to miss the trio of beverage cans in the upper right hand corner.[29] Red Bull employs this unconventional approach because it set out, Grabner explains, to engage its target group, knowing that product sales would follow.[30]

American Express might be the last brand to be mentioned in the same breath as Red Bull, but very much like Red Bull, American Express knows who its best customers are. American Express's selectivity of customers is a hallmark of its brand.

Positioned as a financial institution for high-spend individuals and corporations, American Express enjoys a differentiated position in a highly competitive sector. But the Amex brand strength is based on more than status and snobbery. It's a resource allocation strategy that creates a virtuous loop that feeds back into its brand equity. By limiting the number and type of customers it serves, the company is able to develop products, services, and standards tailored to meet its customers' specific needs. Its service personnel get the training and have the charter and resources to go beyond just fixing customer problems to take the extra steps to create personal connections and help customers get more value from the company.[31]

American Express has recently catered particularly to the small business segment of its market, allowing small business owners to manage their expenses, budget for travel, and earn rewards through their charge cards. The company's high-end Platinum and Centurion cards have high annual fees, but offer considerable benefits for frequent travelers, such as $200 in annual credit toward airline baggage fees and access to hundreds of airport lounges all around the world. Small businesses and frequent travelers are profitable segments that American Express makes an extra effort—at the exclusion of others—to get close to.[32]

◆ Tool: Using Needs-States to Identify Target Segments

Market segmentation of the kind that American Express excels at is all about grouping customers in ways that help you meet their needs more effectively. When it's done well, segmentation has tremendous power to drive strategy and tactics—from channel management to product development to service design.

Segmentation research often relies on demographics, purchase behaviors, and dollars spent to identify and quantify the value of different customer groups, but all these criteria are rapidly losing their meaning these days. As touched on in Chapter Two, a "needs-based" segmentation research approach can identify several needs that a single person may have in different situations during the course of the day, which is a much more realistic assessment of buying behavior. That's why I recommend using quantitative survey data and multivariate analysis to cluster customers into needs-based segments of different value by combining their attitudes and usage occasions.

One of the examples offered in Chapter Two showed how, in researching a healthy snack food, we identified such snacking needs-states as "to tide me over," "to treat myself and indulge," and "to enliven a social occasion." The process helped uncover how the "to treat myself and indulge" needs-state was severely underserved by products perceived as "better-for-you" and was a natural fit for the brand, so we jumped on the opportunity to appeal to the segment.

In simple terms, needs-states combine the purchasing attitudes of users with their purchase occasions. For consumer products, attitudes include such purchase considerations as design-consciousness, price-sensitivity, or the desire for innovative products. Purchase occasions vary from impulse purchases to gift giving to indulgence purchases to obligatory purchases.

Needs-based segmentation allows for the fact that most individuals have more than one demand driver for products that they're interested in. For example, I worked with an apparel brand to use a needs-based segmentation analysis to target specific customers' needs for jeans—for example, customers with a "Fashion Forward Style Seeking" attitude had differing needs for their jeans. For some they were for wearing to work, and for others they were for nights out.

By sorting out these different opportunities, we could understand more deeply what people were looking for—and we could determine which of the brand's products met their needs most closely. (Mere attitudinal- or demographic-only segmentation approaches could have identified target market customers, but they would not have provided any insights into customer needs in ways that would help the company improve the product and contribute to building the brand identity.)

Once we had this data in hand, we were able to quantify the market size of each need. Then we prioritized the ones with the highest potential business value, based on size of market, number of pairs owned, discretionary spending levels, and price sensitivity. Most important, we also prioritized them in order of strongest *brand fit*. (Does attitude fit the brand personality? Does the occasion fit the product design?)

From there, the company was able to use the target segment insights to plan its product lineup, give designers specific styling directions, and place the various products in their appropriate channels and accounts. It designed product displays and in-store styling to show off complete outfits for different needs, and produced communications that spoke directly to specific needs, with advertising that featured products appropriate for a night out in an evening occasion versus a similar product presented in a more casual setting. Everything the company did to market its jeans was targeted at the brand's ideal customer segments, so as to present the right products to the right customers at the moments when they were most likely to be shopping for their particular needs.

Research of this kind allows you to start sifting for insights as soon as you've finished cataloguing all the various needs-states related to your product category. For a nutritional supplement, we identified as many as a dozen needs-states at the start of our research. Of those, we determined that three needs-states in particular were well-aligned with the brand position and product attributes, while most of the others were better aligned with competitors' offerings.

So we focused our strategies on appealing to people in those three needs-states. One of the needs-states that favored our product was "a quick pick-me-up while on the go." We had already been working on developing a single-serve packaging option, and this segmentation insight prompted us to fast-track the new offering and introduce a line of "to go" products. It was the kind of strategic follow-through that wouldn't have been possible through traditional demographic segmentation.

Ultimately, the benefit of the needs-states method is that it reveals which of your customers' emotional drivers are most powerful in relation to your products. Most segmentation analyses are heavy on the "what" (customer behavior) but weak on the "why" (attitudes and motivations that stimulate behavior). Great brands develop lasting, ongoing relationships with their highest-value customer segments, as opposed to the more typical transactional or tactical relationships that mainstream marketing generates. Demographic and behavioral segmentation simply doesn't provide the depth of understanding that creates lasting relationships, which are built by delivering total customer experiences that address customers' core needs.

Creating a Brand-Centered Customer Strategy

No matter how a company pursues its research in segmenting and targeting, the most effective customer strategies are those that integrate the company's brand identity and engage the brand-as-business approach. The managers of great brands put their brands at the center of their customer strategies because that's how they shape expectations and invite like-minded people to engage with them. Brand-based targeting strategies not only enable companies to attract people who share their mindset and values, they also produce clarity and conviction in the management of the business.

This unified brand-as-business strategy maximizes the impact of the brand on your customers, which in turn maximizes return on your brand as an asset. As Tim Suther notes in *Advertising Age*, "Brands must continually strive to increase the value of their customer portfolio at every interaction. Said another way, optimizing the value of individual customer relationships optimizes the overall value of your brand."[33]

In this regard, the Virgin brand has set new standards for the rest of the business world to follow. Virgin uses its brand to drive customer targeting, service, and experience, and in doing so, it has become known as the customers' champion. Virgin goes out of its way to relieve customers of the sacrifices they have had to make while dealing with large, impersonal category leaders in a wide range of industries. The company has fielded dozens of challenger brands, each of which does business with a spirit of fun, innovation, and daring.

Even the provocative name, Virgin, was chosen by founder Richard Branson to represent the brand ideal of entering each new industry category with virginal innocence about what might be possible. Before deciding to invade a new market, Virgin determines whether its unique brand approach would offer something truly different, and whether it might profit from shaking up a relatively static market. Before Virgin invests in an upstart challenger in any industry, it looks to five criteria that would qualify it for the Virgin label: it must be high-quality, it must be innovative, it must challenge existing alternatives, it must provide good value for the money, and it must have a sense of fun. "With these core values as the common thread," wrote Glenn Rifkin in *Strategy+Business* back in 1998, "Mr. Branson has entered one business after another in which he perceived a customer set that was being underserved by a fat and complacent dominant player."[34]

Virgin has in essence functioned as a branded venture capital fund, investing in companies that wear the Virgin label as they enter industries that have included airlines, mobile phones, banking, health clubs, credit cards, and dozens of others. Branson has claimed that securing consumer trust in all these companies is a

Virgin imperative.[35] The mobile phone company bills don't have hidden charges. The credit card agreements are easy to understand. The health club memberships don't involve lengthy contracts. Virgin's brand mission is to offer customers a break from the frustrations of business-as-usual.

In Branson's own words, "If you are seizing on a new business opportunity, deliberately move your customers' expectations up a few notches and consistently over-deliver on your promises—you will leave your competitors struggling to catch up."[36]

◆ Tool: Building a Brand Platform with a Competitive Brand Positioning

Virgin's success across such a diverse array of product lines is a testament to the strength of Virgin's strategic brand platform. Just as a political candidate or group has a platform that outlines the beliefs that drive the campaign, a brand should be based on a platform stating what it represents and what it intends to accomplish.

Two elements make up a strategic brand platform. The first is the brand identity—what the brand stands for. The second is the competitive brand positioning—how the brand compares to and competes with other options in the marketplace. Chapter Six discusses brand identity; here I explain competitive brand positioning, since it is a framework that great brands use to focus their differentiating light and shine it brightly to attract like-minded customers.

Clarifying your competitive brand positioning is essential to brand building because it defines who you are selling to, what your business scope is, and what you do to create value for your customers. Since all three of these factors are in constant flux, your competitive brand positioning should be regularly revisited and updated as needed. No matter how steadfast your commitment to your brand values, how you are different and how you compete can change from one season to the next.

The following is frequently used as a framework for expressing one's competitive brand positioning:

*For **X**, we are the **A** who does **B**, because **C**.*

In this structure, "X" is your target audience, "A" is your frame of reference, "B" is the unique value you deliver, and "C" is the reason or reasons why consumers should believe that you deliver that value.

Here is the competitive brand positioning statement for a national health-oriented restaurant chain:

For everyone who chooses to do something good for themselves (X),

our brand is the convenient place for (A),

great-tasting healthy products that energize the way you live and feel (B)

because we are considerate of what you put in your body, we make it enjoyable to be healthy, and we help create healthier communities (C).

Each element in this framework has a variety of considerations. For "X," your target audience, it's not uncommon to view everyone as a potential customer—who would say they want to turn away business from a viable prospect?! The objective of stipulating a specific target segment or segments is to ensure the time, money, and energy you devote to attracting customers is not so diffuse as to be ineffective. And, as American Express has shown, some customers are worth more than others—they either spend more in your category or they influence the purchase decisions of many others, so you want to target your efforts on them. Also, demographic and income variables lack the predictive power that guide great brands because people's lifestyles and values vary so much. A target segment is distinguished more clearly by a common attitude or need, so your competitive brand positioning should describe your target's attitudinal and needs-based attributes.

For "A," your frame of reference, consider this factor to be the "mental file folder" you want consumers to put you in. Be careful with your scope in this respect. Usually competitive positioning takes place within your industry category, but remember that people often make purchase choices outside narrow categories. Many purchase decisions involve *indirect competition*, in which consumers ask themselves: Juice or soda? Dinner or movie? Vacation or new car? So, as prescribed in Chapter Two, you want to think broadly about what business you're really in and which of your fiercest competitors may lie outside your category.

For "B," the unique value you deliver is the thing that you do for people that no one does as well as you—or no one does at all. This should convey the relevance of your brand to your target customers and its differentiation from others in your frame of reference. You explain your relevance most clearly and astutely when the features and attributes of your offering are translated into customer benefits and values. For example, the technical fabrication of Lululemon products may not be relevant to most people, but the fact that it makes the products look and feel as comfortable as their own skin is. Your brand differentiation also must be clear and meaningful. To craft a differentiating competitive brand positioning, avoid relying on benefits that are common or expected in the category and instead illuminate what sets your brand apart. And remember to avoid an -er positioning, as discussed in Chapter Three. Your unique value shouldn't be based on being small-er, bigg-er, thinn-er, light-er, fast-er, sexi-er, or cheap-er than another brand.

Finally, for "C," you want to remember just how savvy customers have become. They are unlikely to accept your claims about your brand at face value. So in "C" you need to point to evidence—the real reasons why people should believe that you really do provide that unique value referenced in "B." You need to give customers some substantiation they can see or touch, feel and understand to make your claim credible. Perhaps your product incorporates proprietary technology, or you're used and endorsed by experts, or your company has longevity and history. Remember, your claims must stand up to the scrutiny of today's consumers, who have the tools and access to verify them.

A chain of fitness clubs uses the following competitive brand positioning: "*For busy working professionals who have limited time for exercise, we are the all-in-one exercise destination that makes it easy to have a full fitness experience in less than an hour. Our clubs are open 24/7, conveniently located, and equipped with machines that provide a fast, no-hassle fitness experience.*" In this case, the competitive brand positioning specifies the type of customers that the club is geared toward, using lifestyle and attitudinal dimensions. It also indicates other options that the club competes with—not just other clubs, but other exercise activities like working out on home gym equipment and engaging in outdoor sports. And the positioning explains what the club does for customers better than any other option and points to specific proof-points.

Three Ways to Differentiate

The differentiating power of your competitive brand positioning is so important, it's worth delving into further—especially in light of the way many companies have tried to use price to differentiate themselves in the sluggish postrecession economy. Aggressive pricing tactics can't sustainably differentiate your business. To establish meaningful and lasting differentiation, pursue one or more of three chief strategies: Be first. Own an attribute. Specialize. Great brands often lay claim to all three.

Be First. When you are "first to market"—first to create a demand and fill it—your brand achieves a strong differentiating advantage of the market leadership position—whether it's real or perceived. That's why everyone knows the iPad but very few people have even heard of the Motorola Xoom even though some experts said Motorola's was the superior product. "First to market" can mean being the first brand in a given geographic area, but more often being first is based on offering a new type of product, a new service, or a new customer experience. By strongly promoting your brand as "the first," your competitors are challenged to make moves that don't seem outdated, predictable, imitative, or just plain boring in comparison.

Own an Attribute. Once you move beyond the most common customer expectations for friendly service, fair prices, and quality products, you have a world of attributes for differentiation: big, small, fast, fun, easy, surprising, safe, soft. . . . Your goal should be to identify a brand attribute that no one else is talking about or one that constitutes a serious weakness for your main competitor—and then adopt it as the defining attribute for your brand. Target long ago decided to use design to differentiate its brand from Walmart, knowing that Walmart's obsession with low prices almost precluded competition on that basis. Owning an attribute requires you to overdeliver on it and communicate it at every touchpoint. Customer expectations for everything at Target now center on design. If you own a meaningful attribute, people are more likely to remember you and have a compelling reason to consider you.

Specialize. Perhaps the most effective means to differentiate your brand and avoid chasing customers is to specialize in a target market. By designing your business to appeal specifically to a type of customer, you become known as an expert for that market. Here's what I mean: A Google search for website agencies in my city yielded eight thousand results, which may represent at least a hundred agencies that all offer the same undifferentiated range of services—effective, innovative, well-designed websites. But then there's City Gates, an agency that specializes in building websites for churches. The people at City Gates have developed deep expertise in the kinds of features, content, and designs that church members want and need. This expertise separates them from the crowd of other web service providers. If you were responsible for picking a website vendor for your church, which agency would you pick—the one who specializes in serving organizations like yours or one of the other very competent but generic web agencies?

Humans are genetically hardwired to notice differences, and differences are often what attract people to your brand in the first place. Brands that stand out for customers—lighthouse brands— are powered by strong and clear differentiation.

Reviving a Running Shoe Brand

When I worked with a running shoe company that had taken on the aggressive goal of doubling sales within five years, we all recognized the company needed to clarify its brand platform internally so the organization would know how to stay on track during the growth phase. In the course of adding new markets, new products, new acquisitions, and new people, the company would need to ensure that its brand position was expressed and delivered clearly to customers so that the full differentiation of the brand would be better understood and properly valued.

I led company leaders through a series of work sessions in which we covered elemental questions such as, Who are the best customers for our brand? What competitive position has the greatest relevance to and differentiation for our chosen targets and that we can consistently deliver? What differentiators give us the greatest competitive advantage? What do we have to start, change, or stop doing in order to really deliver on our brand identity and competitive positioning?

Company leaders were concerned that the brand's existing position was dangerously fragile. Despite robust sales, the brand was developing a public image as being for older, less trendy, and less savvy consumers. The leaders wanted to the brand to "get younger" and become more dynamic, stylish, and contemporary. They also determined that the most fruitful approach would be to appeal to "endorsers"—the running elite, from whom other consumers take their cues about what's hot, and urban consumers, who drive lifestyle trends.

Through consumer research, we learned that the urban consumer wanted quality and top-notch product performance features such as cushioning and traction, even though the people in this segment had no intention of actually using the product for performance. These needs fit with the company's capabilities in developing superior performance technology and with the brand's origins in medical products—and they were needs shared by the running elite target segment. My client concluded that as long as they appealed to the running elite, the brand would have credibility with the urban consumer.

Then, to appeal to the running elite, the brand had to be perceived as more athletic, performance based—and as an innovator and leader in the category. Although the company had the products and technology to support these desired perceptions, it hadn't been communicating them effectively. And for both targets, the brand needed to resonate emotionally. Urban consumers align with brands that are leaders in culture and coolness. Elite runners want to buy brands with identities that resonate with their passion for running.

We considered several different positioning options, using insights from a Competitive Landscape Map like the one described in Chapter Two and a Brand Diagnostic evaluation from Chapter Three. We concluded that while most other brands in the category were promoting the superior technology of their footwear, we would position our brand on *fit*—in both the rational and emotional senses of the word. The rational aspects of fit involved technical shoe design and cushioning. The emotional aspects of fit involved styling and coolness—shoes that you *can* wear for performance, but ones that you *want* to wear for their look and image. In our research consumers told us that this positioning would be very differentiating. It would be ownable.

From this strategic foundation, we developed the following competitive brand positioning: "Only we design performance solutions that fit athletes who are confident in themselves and are driven to achieve." We also listed the reasons for believing this statement, derived from product attributes, company history, and production capabilities.

Though the positioning statement breaks from strict order of the X+A+B+C framework, all the essential elements are there. The brand's target population was athletes who are confident in themselves and driven to achieve. The frame of reference was performance solutions, because although our focus was footwear, we knew our target also spent a lot on other products and categories that enhanced their performance and that we were competing for overall share of wallet. The unique brand value was design and fit.

This statement, along with brand essence (discussed in Chapter Six) formed the strategic platform for the brand. This platform in turn was used to drive and guide all business strategies and plans. For example, we used it to develop a brand image board that shaped all visual communication. The board contained pictures of confident, driven athletes who would convey the emotional brand appeal, along with close-ups of product details to convey the unique design and fit. Product designers responded by focusing more carefully on the fit of products, and by doubling down on getting sizing and styling right so the products lived up to the new expectations.

The company fast-tracked product launches targeted to athletes rather than more mainstream consumers. And the advertising campaign was changed, too, from one that had been solely emotional in appeal to one that supported the emotional appeal with substantive claims to support the new shoes' quality and fit. From the bottom to the top, the company's relationship with its product—and thus, with its customers—was transformed when the leadership took a hard look at evaluating what its brand platform had to offer.

Great Brands Employ Brand Attraction

Brand managers who chase customers may believe they're doing the smart thing, seeking to maximize the breadth of customer appeal, but they are often taking risks that aren't always clear to see. Chasing customers can drive down profits, blur your brand message, and, especially for retailers and other experience-oriented businesses, put your truly loyal and valuable customers at the end of the line behind people who aren't now and never will be counted among your fans.

Whether it's Lululemon, American Express, or the Rolling Stones, great brands all share a clear vision of themselves: an internal culture strong enough to resist temptations to stray from the vision in the quest for more customers. As Richard Branson puts it, "Our customers and investors relate to us more as an idea or philosophy than as a company. We offer the Virgin experience, and make sure it is consistent across all sectors. It's all about the brand."[37] With brand-centered strategic approaches to their businesses, the leaders of great brands are able to position their brands in ways that play to their strengths, so that even customers who are not looking for them will find them anyway, like lighthouses in the fog.

CHAPTER 5

Great Brands Sweat the Small Stuff

Marketers at the Procter & Gamble Company (P&G) coined the term "FMOT" in 2005. Pronounced eff-mot, it stands for "First Moment of Truth"—the three to seven seconds when a shopper notices an item in a retail environment. According to P&G managers, the FMOT is crucial because in that instant, a shopper will decide to either pick up a product or pass it by. P&G was so committed to the importance of FMOT that it created a new position, Director of First Moment of Truth, heading a fifteen-person FMOT department assisted by fifty FMOT leaders stationed around the world.[1]

Dina Howell, P&G's first FMOT director, told the *Wall Street Journal* in 2006 that P&G believed its product packaging design should "interrupt" shoppers' attention in some very particular ways. P&G developed a set of questions that each package design must answer: "Who am I? What am I? Why am I right for you?"[2] Then, that same design must function in the home in the important second moment of truth, when the customer uses the product. By conducting about twenty thousand studies involving an estimated five million consumers in nearly a hundred countries, P&G continually refines this consumer-centric approach to package design.[3]

When P&G's Pantene, the world's leading hair care brand, came up for a redesign, the new packages were designed for impact at both moments of truth. Market research showed that although Pantene products were categorized in "collections" for normal, dry, or oily hair, customers were often misdiagnosing their own hair, and not buying the right kind of Pantene as a result. So new collections were designed around people's desired effect—volume, curly hair, or straight hair, for instance. The lettering on the new packaging highlighted Pantene's distinctive ProV vitamin content in high-gloss, metallic lettering. The designers also retained Pantene's previous innovation, in which conditioner bottles were made with their caps on the bottom, in so-called tottles that help the highly viscous conditioner escape the spout faster. When the redesign was finished, Pantene was shipped in brighter, more attractive packaging that was easier to identify in the store and easier to use at home.[4]

Such great attention to detail in package design is just the start for great brands. Managers of great brands view *every* consumer contact with the brand as an occasion that might either enhance the brand's value or undermine it. They continuously seek out opportunities for brand expression in even the finest details of execution, because they know that each interaction, each touchpoint, communicates a valuable message.

The people behind great brands need to think big, but they try not to let those big thoughts distract them from sweating the small stuff. All the little things you do—or fail to do—for your customers in person will out-communicate the big things you may claim through mass media. Few advertising or marketing messages can ever be as impressive, distinctive, and memorable as a one-on-one brand experience that's been designed down to the last detail and manages to appeal to most if not all of the five human senses.

Yet even a single extraordinary experience is only the starting point. Great brands align and unify all their customer experiences, overcoming organizational silos and adopting a customer point of view, because customers expect seamless brand experiences over time and across channels. And ultimately, they seize the opportunity to apply attention to detail in the actual running of the business. This chapter outlines how great brands progress—first sweating the small stuff in packaging, then in every touchpoint and every detail, then across all customer experiences and every aspect of operations.

Speaking Through Design

Great brands such as those from P&G often try to speak first through product and packaging design, because design has such a direct and immediate personal impact on the customer. A signature design language in your product and its packaging can convey the unique meaning and value of the brand through your customer's intimate firsthand experience. Since we respond to design with our emotions, design is one of the most important ways to make the emotional connections described in Principle Two, "Great Brands Avoid Selling Products."

In the best-selling biography by Walter Isaacson, Steve Jobs credited Mike Markkula, one of Apple's early investors, with impressing upon him the importance of form in relation to function. "[Mike] taught me that people do judge a book by its cover," Jobs said.[5] From the handle on the first iMacs to the signature white color of the iPod's headphones to the roundedness of the iPad's bottom edge, all of Apple's products adhere to a philosophy of simplicity, craftsmanship, and user empathy. Apple's lead designer Jony Ive also recalls spending a lot of time with Jobs on the packaging of Apple products. "I love the process of unpacking something," he says. "You design a ritual of unpacking to make the product feel special. Packaging can be theater, it can create a story."[6]

Apple may be the best-known brand that speaks through design, but a design ethos is what helps lesser-known brands make a big impression on customers. Chobani, a rising star on the packaged goods horizon, uses design to stand out and create a memorable experience out of a simple activity—eating yogurt. CEO Hamdi Ulukaya explains that as a start-up Chobani couldn't afford to advertise, so the product packaging became almost as important as the yogurt itself. Ulukaya designed his package in the form of a European-style cup, which makes for a squatter, fatter tub that looks bigger than others. Also, he didn't want the painted-on labels used by other yogurt brands; he preferred shrunken-on sleeves because they projected sharper colors. "People say, 'It's yogurt, who cares?' But there's emotion to it," he says. "You can make this a moment: the opening of it, the eating of it, the experience. I spent so much time on every single detail." It's not a stretch to credit this Jobs-esque obsession with design as one of the drivers behind Chobani's rise to more than $1 billion in revenues in less than five years.[7]

Brand Expression Is in the Details

Some of the most memorable brand experiences are created by deft choices in design. Ron Rogowski, Forrester Research's principal analyst on customer experience, encourages companies to use a mix of senses in all design, including web design. "Interactions that engage users fulfill their emotional needs," he writes. "If firms want to keep [online] users interested, they need to enrich the sensory experience. While Web experiences don't allow users to taste or smell objects, they can and absolutely should engage users' senses of sight, hearing, and even touch."[8] Whether through product design, web design, or retail design, great brands create worlds that appeal to all our senses, and use details and decor to help express their brand personalities.

The online retailer UncommonGoods does better than most to engage website visitors emotionally through its multimedia site design. Personable product stories, relaying the artist who conceived the product or pointing out details that enhance enjoyment of it, accompany each item listing. Videos show you what products do once they've been turned on. Before you buy an alarm clock, you can hear what it sounds like. The company also creates an engaging experience by inviting customers to vote on which new products make it to the pages of its site.[9] UncommonGoods lives up to its brand name and stands out from others by offering an immersive and entertaining shopping experience over the Internet.

Smells, though usually overlooked, are a particularly powerful design detail in brick-and-mortar experiences. The management at Starwood Hotels and Resorts created distinctive, patented smells for each of the company's hotel brands.[10] As the company's chief executive in 2006, Steven Heyer explained the scents are part of the company's comprehensive effort to make an emotional connection with guests and cultivate preference and brand loyalty that would generate "industry leading RevPar (revenue per available room), footprint growth, and Return On Invested Capital."[11]

Even H&R Block, by no means a great brand, has discovered how the smell emanating from a freshly brewed pot of coffee kept in reception areas makes a positive impact on the mood of customers who are likely to be anxious while awaiting their appointments with tax preparers.[12] When you walk into a Williams-Sonoma store, you often get a feeling of having walked into a kitchen filled with the aroma of good cooking, thanks to the store's food prep demonstrations. Food samples are frequently offered, as well, making a visit to Williams-Sonoma a full-sensory experience.

At their best, retail brands use store design to take a fresh approach to architecture, floor layout, surface materials, and fixtures to create a brand world of sorts. With a signature design language to make that critical emotional connection with customers, customers experience the attributes and dimensions of the brand through design. Trader Joe's use of wooden display cases, hand-drawn signs, and Hawaiian shirted and tattooed employees bring to life the quirky personality, sense of discovery, and savvy customer targeting that forms its brand platform. Even the chain's direct mail piece, the newsprint *Fearless Flyer*, conveys the brand's unpretentious character. All these design cues lead to greater brand understanding and affinity and elevate shopping at Trader Joe's from a grocery store trip to a cultural experience.

Bringing the REI Brand to Life

At REI, the outdoor sporting goods company, store designs include walk-in freezers for testing sleeping bags and indoor climbing walls and faux mountainsides for testing footwear. Some stores provide areas for trying out gas cookers and setting up tents, too. The company stores express the brand mission of outdoor excitement and adventure through design and layout, signage and graphics, fixtures and materials—right down to the ice-pick door handles.

"We used to be product-driven—assuming we have the experience in gear and relying on customers to trust us to pick the right products," former CEO Sally Jewell explained to *Fast Company* back in 2004. But the organization had a breakthrough in 2000 and shifted "to being market-driven—paying attention to who these customers are and how we can adapt to the way they want to recreate."[13]

The 2012 opening of REI's 39,000-square-foot store in a historic building in lower Manhattan was a departure for a company that had always built retail locations from the ground up. Designers worked inside the first three floors of the 130-year-old Puck Building to bring out the inherent industrial-age beauty of the structure. Painted brickwork and iron columns were stripped to reveal their true materials. Painted wood floors were sanded down and recycled or reclaimed. Two fourteen-foot cast iron fly-wheels (once used to run printing presses in the building) were reclaimed and put on proud display, protruding right up through the sales floor.

"Our interest in stewardship of the land is reflected in the way we have taken stewardship of the store," says Jewell. Their hope, she explains, is that by bringing the Puck Building back to life, the store will help people understand the REI brand and its core value of authenticity, "being true to the outdoors." A glass railing surrounding the main staircase has been etched with a topographical map of Manhattan. "The message is," Jewell adds, "the outdoors is right around the corner in New York."[14]

Design should always be taken up as the fundamental first step toward the ultimate ideal: memorable customer experiences of your brand. Great brands seek out opportunities for brand expression in even the finest details of execution. The culture at REI embraces this notion, with its commitment to leaving no detail unattended in the experience of its brand.

Even the tiniest of gestures can make a memorable impression. I still remember flipping over a reloadable charge card from Caribou Coffee and seeing fun, uplifting messages printed on the back, including nice thoughts like "Hold hands, not grudges," and intriguing ones, too, like the one that said simply, "Yes, it is possible."

It's easy to miss or miscalculate the value of brand touch-points such as these. They are pieces of unused branding real estate that most people wouldn't give a second thought, like the postage stamp promoting efficient lighting on a piece of mail from an environmental group (how appropriate!) or the water decanter in the Minnesota restaurant that provided this reassur-ing note: *"Fresh water compliments of the house. This double filtered water is free of impurities, free of wasteful packaging, and free of charge.*" (How refreshing!)

These little details in brand expression were hardly necessary—we've all used charge cards featuring logos or fanciful designs, been served water from unlabeled decanters, and received letters with ordinary stamps. I doubt I would have noticed their absence if they hadn't been there. But I did notice them, and they did have an impact on me. Each made a positive brand impression. And that's the point. Conventional wisdom says that there are only a few ways that customers get exposed to your brand—advertising, packaging, websites, and social media. But in reality, your brand has hundreds of touchpoints with the outside world. In each of these cases, those small spaces could have been left blank or, worse, marred with a logo or a crass advertising message. Instead, these far-sighted brands used those touchpoints as opportunities to make statements that reflect their core values and convey a sense of their personality.

Valuing the Customer Experience

The risk of calling attention to such brand touchpoints is that I may seem to be suggesting an unhealthy obsession with details. However, the mark of a great brand is not being obsessive compulsive; it is being intentional. Great brands are purposeful in everything they do. They meticulously design the experiences of their brand touchpoints because that's how brand vision gets translated into customer reality. They know that executing on the brand strategy with excellence throughout the entire customer experience builds their brand integrity and impact.

Business leaders generally underestimate the power of experience. Brand management firm Prophet released a State of the Market study in 2011 showing that only 13 percent of executives believe the purchase experience is the most critical driver of future brand equity, whereas 36 percent said product and service quality would be the top driver.[15]

Most marketing executives think about customer experience, but they also acknowledge that their companies don't value it as a critical component of the brand and develop it as a core competency. According to a study by the Chartered Institute of Marketing, seven out of ten of marketers believe that investing in customer experience is more effective than investing in marketing communications, but only 13 percent believe that their company "excels" at delivering a day-to-day brand experience that matches up to what the brand promises. A third of organizations were found to not use their own brand guidelines, while half didn't have customer experience or employee brand behavior guidelines at all.[16] Managers seem to continue to emphasize product quality and attributes, failing to acknowledge that the entire experience—and every detail in it—shapes customer perceptions of the brand.

Shaking executives out of their myopia takes some effort. A brand revitalization effort I led for a fast food chain began with a special work session for the executive leadership team. The goal of the session was to help everyone make an honest assessment of the brand execution as expressed through customer experience. For most of the work sessions I lead, I assign special tasks for the participants to undertake prior to the session. For this particular client, the tasks involved making a series of restaurant visits with specific instructions to follow.

One task was to visit the same restaurant location at various times of day and night, to help the participants assess the consistency of the customer experience. Another task was to bring a friend along on some visits and ask the friend to complete an assessment of the experience, to help the executives see things that an insider might miss. The final step was to visit the restroom at a restaurant and sit on the toilet, to get a truly authentic experience of the facilities. We believed this step—essentially telling the CEO and her executive team to "take a crap" where their customers have to go—would be a real eye-opener, and indeed it was!

When the work session began, participants shared their stories and pictures (part of the assignment), which revealed just how poor their brand's customer experience was. The CEO admitted that she usually sampled the company's food by visiting the drive-thru window. Because her attention had focused on the product, she had rarely been inside their dining rooms and it had been years since she visited a restroom, much less sat on a toilet. By following the detailed pre-work instructions, she and her colleagues had to confront how dirty and unkempt their locations were—a truth they had heard many times before but didn't internalize and accept until they experienced it themselves. All their sobering reports were uncomfortable to hear, but their collective frustration helped give us a much-needed grounding in what was wrong with the brand. When difficult issues arose, no one felt the issues could be sidestepped. The restaurant visits had provided them all with a common understanding of the company's customer experience problems, which made it easier for them to commit to solutions.

Experiencing Your Brand Like a Customer

If you want to understand your brand through your customers' experiences, you've got to put your brand to the test. It might be surprising how seldom company decision makers subject themselves to the same treatment their customers receive, but, as with the restaurant CEO in the restroom, it often requires an intentional and deliberate undertaking to dole out and complete these kinds of assignments.

For an e-retailer, I asked the company president to order a product online and have it delivered to his home. That sounds simple, but most executives never see what the product and its packaging looks like after it leaves the warehouse, takes a cross-country ride with the USPS, and gets dumped on a doorstep. And yet, in a study by IBM, nearly three-quarters of the respondents cited a retailer's ability to deliver a positive postpurchase experience as an important consideration in whether or not to recommend the retailer to others. Consumers now look for a flawless and seamless experience from researching to buying to receiving delivery of a product.[17]

For restaurant brands, the assignment I give often involves ordering items with the lowest sales mix. That's because sampling some of the least popular menu items gives a sense of what a product is like when the ingredients have been sitting around for a while and the chef or crew don't have the proficiency that comes from making and serving the product frequently. Most executives try the newest products on the menu or have favorites they always order.

For any services company, it's an eye-opening experience for an executive to pick up the phone and make a complaint. A CEO can learn a lot from enduring a sixty-second wait time (which doesn't sound that bad until you have to sit there listening to bad hold music), trying to converse with a live representative (who may or may not have the skills, tools, authority, or inclination to fix the problem), and seeing how the complaint is (or isn't) resolved. Corporate executives set and review service procedures and some might occasionally listen in on service calls, but nothing illuminates the customer experience like personally dialing up that 800 number.

Going the Second Mile at Chick-fil-A

Perhaps these assignments wouldn't be necessary if every brand had customer-service details baked into its operations the way fast-food franchisor Chick-fil-A has. Chick-fil-A's program of "Second Mile Service" raises the concept of customer service to literally religious heights. The "second mile" is a reference to the Biblical counsel that "whoever compels you to go one mile, go with him two."[18]

Second Mile Service aims to provide a service level you'd expect to receive at finer establishments, because Chick-fil-A's brand is grounded in exceeding customer expectations. When you thank an employee, the response you will always receive is "my pleasure" (not "no problem" or even "you're welcome"). Chick-fil-A employees roam the dining room, offering to refill guests' drinks—and in the restrooms they fold down the corners of the toilet paper so it's clear they're paying attention to the brand experience there.

The company spends more than $1 million annually sweating the small stuff: quarterly research gives every restaurant a two-page report that shows how it's performing relative to the brand standards and to the chain's top performers.[19] This attention to detail has been rewarded by some of the best financials in the industry and by awards that include "Top Large Chain" in Zagat's fast food survey and "Top Restaurant Brand" in J.D. Power and Associates restaurant satisfaction study.[20]

The company's commitment to experience excellence is supported by rigorous recruitment and training practices. CEO Dan Cathy claims Chick-fil-A spends more on staff training than any other restaurant chain. Cathy boasts of his company's 80 percent retention rate among hourly employees (compared to the average fast food chain turnover rate of more than 200 percent) and credits those numbers to the tight controls kept on who gets to wear a Chick-fil-A nametag.[21] A favorite saying at the corporate office is "It's easier to get a job in the CIA than at Chick-fil-A."[22]

◆ Tool: Visualizing Your Brand Touchpoints

So if you wanted to replicate Chick-fil-A's success, how would you get your arms around all the little details of your brand's touchpoints? Developing a Brand Touchpoint Wheel is a great place to start. With a Brand Touchpoint Wheel, you can have at your fingertips a visual representation of all your brand touchpoints, along with the impact various stakeholder groups have on them.

To assemble a Brand Touchpoint Wheel, first audit all the ways your company communicates with the outside world and all the experiences your company provides. This can seem like a Herculean task, but if you assemble a cross-functional team to conduct the audit, the process is more manageable and you'll get more comprehensive results.

You can organize your audit by interactions with customers before purchase, at purchase, and after purchase and then add noncustomer interactions like corporate touchpoints—or you might classify your audit results by static touchpoints like advertising or packaging, human touchpoints like call centers or salespeople, and interactive touchpoints like social media or websites. Or group touchpoints according to those the company controls and those that it merely influences. Remember to include your products themselves, since they usually have the greatest impact on brand perceptions—and yet are often overlooked as brand touchpoints in this kind of exercise.

Once you've identified all your touchpoints, list the internal departments and processes responsible for each and map out areas where you find commonalities. You'll soon be able to put together a visual wheel that shows your brand in the center, all the touchpoints on the rim, and the different groups that impact the touchpoints as spokes radiating out to them. (See Figure 5.1 for a Brand Touchpoint Wheel template. On the *What Great Brands Do* website, http://WhatGreatBrandsDo.com, you can download this template and access a worksheet to help you create one for your organization.)

Once your Brand Touchpoint Wheel is assembled, you can use it as a tool for ensuring your touchpoints reflect your brand

Figure 5.1 Brand Touchpoint Wheel

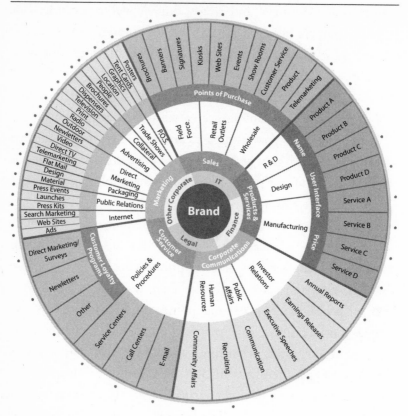

appropriately. Start with customer research, self-assessments, and industry reports to evaluate the experience you deliver at each touchpoint. Compare those evaluations with your brand platform and desired customer experience and it will become clear which touchpoints are out of alignment. You can also use that data to identify the touchpoints that have the most impact on key stakeholders' expectations and experiences. Also look at the size of the gap between how you're performing today and how you should be, the cost of making improvements, and how much the touchpoint could affect your company's longer-term goals and objectives.

From all this data, you can identify the touchpoints you need to focus on—and for each touchpoint you designate as a priority, develop an action plan for optimizing it, measuring your improvements, and managing it on an ongoing basis.

Breaking Down Organizational Silos

When I was at Sony, we used a Brand Touchpoint Wheel to raise internal awareness of the importance of brand expression outside traditional advertising and promotional efforts, and ultimately to improve that expression in several key areas.

Assembling the cross-functional team to conduct the initial touchpoint audit was a significant undertaking in and of itself. Initially, the selected representatives from departments like Legal and Facilities were dubious about their participation in the effort. But as the team started to collect and collate examples from different touchpoints, everyone began to recognize how many different ways the outside world came into contact with the brand—and soon, team members were unearthing brand touchpoints we would never have considered, such as the hold music on our corporate phone system (since Sony owned a major record label, we could have been featuring popular or emerging artists instead of running a generic track) and the collateral inserted into the boxes when products were shipped to customers (the heavily promotional offers detracted from Sony's premium brand image).

The employee recruitment ads we used at job fairs, for example, hadn't been on anyone's radar outside the recruiting staff until the touchpoint wheel team worked through all the ways in which prospective employees encountered the brand. We realized that the ads designed to solicit applications from interested job-seekers served as powerful brand touchpoints because they were highly visible to potential customers (as with many companies, Sony employees are often customers first) and because they were intended to attract applicants who would fit the corporate culture and align with the brand values.

When we conducted our initial audit, we saw that the existing recruitment ads were uninspired and undifferentiated. They communicated a standard message about the company's reputation that really any brand in the technology sector could have run. They weren't bad, per se, but they missed the opportunity to convey a more meaningful and compelling brand message. As we went through the prioritization process and gap analysis, we became convinced that a different approach was needed. So we guided and supported the Human Resources department in developing a new recruitment campaign that aligned with the Sony brand essence, "We create technologies that inspire people to dream and find joy." The new ads featured headlines like "Dreams Wanted" and included provocative images melding people and our products.

The new ads passed the important internal litmus test, as existing employees indicated the ads resonated with them—and they stood out to prospective employees. Not only did we see an increase in the number of applications responding to the campaign, but also the types of applicants who responded seemed to be more in line with the kind of employee we had been seeking. Moreover, our work in this area increased understanding of the impact of brand touchpoints beyond consumer advertising campaigns throughout the Sony workforce, and it led to the optimization of other previously overlooked yet significant touchpoints.

A Brand Touchpoint Wheel is a great tool for opening people's eyes to the reality that everyone in an organization has a responsibility to interpret and reinforce the brand appropriately. In the end you'll have a tool and action plans that align all your brand touchpoints and ensure a consistent brand experience in every contact with your company.

Pursuing the Seamless
Customer Experience

Every brand shares an inherent operational problem: The customer expects a seamless brand experience, but large companies need to operate to some extent in organizational silos, delineated by function. The result? Employees often make decisions and take actions within their silos, with little regard for their impact on the customer experience in total.

"[I]t's the unusual organization that's set up to let people think and act collectively on behalf of customers," writes customer experience consultant Jeanne Bliss. Despite customers' across-the-board interactions with companies, "the typical silo structure bumps the customer disjointedly . . . the customer becomes the grand guinea pig, experiencing each variation of an organization's ability, or inability, to work together." This produces, she says, a breeding ground for customers' lack of respect toward and discontent with businesses.[23]

Great brands work at closing this gap between the real and the ideal, so that customers are more likely to get the seamless brand experiences they expect. At REI, the immersive experience of the brand in-store is carried over into other channels. The company's website and social media pages translate the brand mission into visuals, layouts, functionality, and content. Its catalogs, print materials, and e-mail communications are similarly aligned. And each channel promotes cross-channel benefits such as in-store pickup for orders placed on the website and in-store Internet kiosks for easy product lookup.

But this level of alignment didn't just happen. Through detailed audits, the company had identified many disconnects between the in-store and online experience. For example, the information provided about a product in-store would differ dramatically in both style and substance from content about the same product online—even the product image would look dramatically different.[24]

Disconnects like these happen at other companies—different prices and promotional offers in different channels are the most common. They result from different teams working on the various channels. In some cases, separate merchant teams exist for brick-and-mortar and e-commerce and each operates independently.

Consumers no longer tolerate these disconnects. They expect to be able go to a store to pick up the orders they placed on a company's website; they expect store associates to be able to access inventory status in real time and arrange to get the product from a different store or through the website; they expect one price for a product regardless of the channel, and they expect to have the option of price-matching the lowest price when the occasional difference is found; they even expect to be able to return products across channels. These expectations require companies to "sweat the small stuff" enough to overcome organizational barriers and to make the investments in technology, training, and operations required to deliver a seamless, integrated experience.

REI has made a concerted effort to coordinate efforts among its departments so that its customers can switch between channels without disruption or confusion. But the company's success can be attributed primarily to the brand clarity all its people share. "Some folks work very hard on the brand experience," says REI vice president Kevin Hagen, "but it really starts from our core as mission-driven organization. The focus on mission allows the whole organization to have a commitment to the customer and to the outdoors. That is the crux, the center of our experience."[25]

◆ Tool: Using a Customer Experience Architecture to Construct Your Brand Experiences

Try to imagine the customer experience of your brand as a tour through a well-designed house. Turning on the lights, running the hot water, switching on the oven are all done with little or no thought on your part to the functional "silos" behind each of the systems you've engaged with (electric, water, natural gas). The architecture and interior design of the house are executed so well that you are mainly aware only of the house itself.

In a similar way, the tool I call a Customer Experience Architecture can serve the same function of optimizing, prioritizing, and unifying all the customer experiences your brand offers so that each one provides an integrated experience of your brand. A Customer Experience Architecture is a framework for designing and delivering the optimal experiences to different customer segments in different channels. It's an *architecture* similar to other strategic architectures that are used as planning tools, like a brand architecture or an information architecture—or a structural architecture for building a house. (See Figure 5.2. On the *What Great Brands Do* website, http://WhatGreatBrandsDo .com, you can download the Customer Experience Architecture framework and access a worksheet to help you create one.)

A few years ago my husband and I had firsthand experience of trying to design a house for ourselves, and in that process I saw many echoes of the process of designing customer experiences. After all, a house is more than the sum of the materials that go into it. My husband and I were really building our desired *home experience*. Here are the steps for building a Customer Experience Architecture, some of which can be mapped onto the experience of building a house.

1. *The brand platform:* The first thing our architect wanted to understand was our vision for the house. Did we want a home with a lot of character? Or a designer's dream? Or a simple, functional space? A vision of that sort is equivalent to your brand platform, the first step in developing a Customer Experience Architecture. You start by reaffirming what you want your brand

Figure 5.2 Customer Experience Architecture

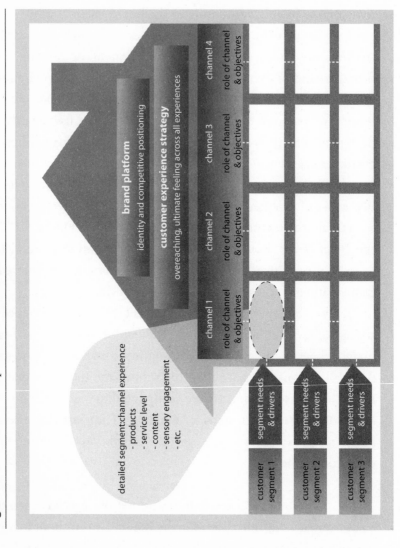

to stand for, the overarching idea that represents you. REI's brand platform is the excitement and adventure of the outdoors; Chick-fil-A's is exceeding customers' expectations with a servant's spirit.

2. *Customer experience strategy:* Then we worked on translating our vision into the overall feeling we desired in our house. Did we want a cocoon for relaxing, a clubhouse for our family to gather in, or an entertainment hub for friends and neighbors? That's the second step—articulating your customer experience strategy, the overall experience you want to deliver across all channels. Perhaps you want to create a place—like Starbucks' "third place"—for customers to discover. Perhaps you want customers to be pampered by legendary service.

3. *Channel requirements and objectives:* Next we needed to look at our specific considerations and priorities for each room in the house. Did we want a wide-open kitchen? A walk-in closet in the bedroom? It was time to consider our budget and the size of our property. In the same way, in developing a Customer Experience Architecture, you express your strategy according to channel or service line. Outline the business requirements and objectives of each and factor in your operational capabilities and assets.

Your website, for example, may use sophisticated filtering technology that makes it easy for customers to find whatever they're looking for. So you may specify that channel for carrying a very broad assortment. Or the location and layouts of your brick-and-mortar stores may be perfect for grab-and-go purchases, so that channel may be all about speed of service.

4. *Customer segments:* The next step is to delineate your target customers. Different target segments have different needs—some may value convenience over price; others may be looking for an entertaining experience. As noted in Chapter Four, the most enlightening and useful strategies segment customers by needs-states—that is, the combination of the prevailing category attitude a customer holds and the specific occasion

in which the product will be used. In the Customer Experience Architecture, outline those different needs-based segments as well as the drivers of purchase decisions and brand perceptions of each. In our home-building process, we had only two people to consider—my husband and me—but our priority "segments" included my husband's needs for a large area for watching TV on a big screen and for a place to tinker with our motorcycle, and my needs for a clear sightline to the kitchen and for a quiet home office space.

5. *Prioritization:* From these last two steps, you can assemble a grid with the channel requirements and objectives as columns and target segments as rows. If we had created a grid for our house plans, my husband's "segment" would have intersected with the "channels" of family room, master bedroom, office, and garage.

Each segment/channel intersection represents a potential source of business and a discrete experience to design and deliver. You should assign values to the different segment/channel inter-sections in your grid so you can prioritize them. Consider the role each plays in reinforcing your brand values and attributes and achieving your desired brand position. Also factor in criteria like profit potential, fit with your long-term strategy, differentiation, and value perceived by customers to determine which experi-ences are the most important. You should also look for synergies between the intersections, where a focus on one intersection might yield improved results in another, as well. Your website might be used by multiple segments with different needs, for example, so you would cover several intersections by prioritizing that channel.

6. *Experience design:* Now outline the ways you are going to meet the segment-specific needs in each channel, either by con-tinuing existing approaches and improving them based on the new insights you've gleaned while creating the architecture, or by developing entirely new ones. These plans are like those that the designer crafted for the different rooms in our house—they

indicated the specific features and designs that would be incorporated to meet our needs.

Use all the levers of customer experience—product, service, content, community, value, facilities, and the rest. What product categories will you feature? Will you do sampling and demonstrations? What added value services will you offer? What information is provided and how? Think about appealing to all five senses to make a visceral impact.

7. *Assessment and integration:* At this point, you'll be able to see your architecture assembled as a whole house and you'll be able to inspect the design for integrity. Ask yourself, will your brand platform be delivered throughout every experience? Do the discrete experiences contribute to your overall customer experience strategy? Do experiences complement and enhance each other, or do they conflict or detract from each other? You may have found a way to inject fun and differentiation into your mobile app by including games, but games may not be appropriate if your overall strategy is about providing a streamlined experience. It may be easy to offer a multitude of products through your website, but if that causes people to expect you to carry all those products in your stores, you may want to rethink your assortment strategy. You may need to go back to the drawing board on your architecture a few times to reconcile conflicts and contradictions.

You also need to show how you will integrate the experiences to ensure that customers get the seamless shopping experience they expect. Use a flowchart or customer experience journey map to depict different customer experiences from the customer point of view. (See Figure 5.3 for an example of a useful flow chart.) Show the steps customers go through as they interact with your company, researching a product, browsing your content, contacting customer service, purchasing from a store, and so on, and what they experience at each step. Show how different experiences feed into and from each other, and how you bridge potential gaps.

Figure 5.3 Customer Experience Architecture Flow Chart

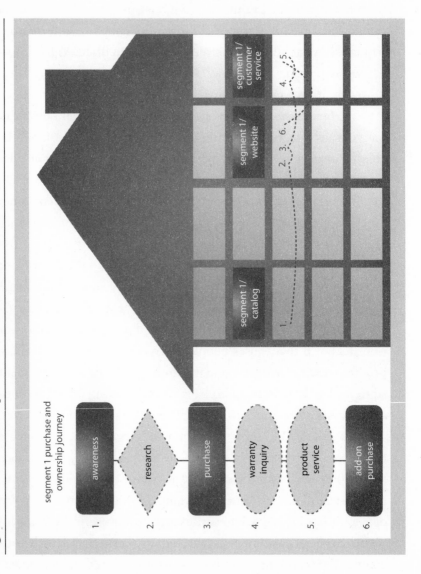

8. *Description:* Finally—once you've ensured your framework has integrity—use narratives, images, idea boards, videos, and any other media you can think of to convey your vision for each priority customer experience and all the granular details that comprise them. You will use these tools to convey your customer experience plan to your stakeholders and help them identify their roles in delivering the plan.

Creating a Customer Experience Architecture isn't rocket science, but it does require a good bit of discipline, dedication, and adherence to the deliberate process. Just as a great house doesn't pop out of the ground of its own accord, great customer experiences don't just happen. If you leave customer experience to chance, chances are your company will produce customer experiences that are bland at best, and occasionally much worse.

Architecting a Multichannel Experience

The return on your investment in a Customer Experience Architecture can be significant. One fitness multichannel retailer used a Customer Experience Architecture to get all its employees, executives, and vendors on the same page about how to increase its competitive advantage in all four of its channels: brick-and-mortar stores, website, catalog and phone order, and e-mail marketing.

For the website, for instance, I helped the company develop the channel objective (step three in the architecture process): "Leverage the personalization capabilities of web technology to provide the most customized, customer-driven experience; a rich content and community resource." For the stores, we determined the channel objective should be "Create a multi-dimensional experience that highlights the brand differentiators and makes the shopping process personal and accessible, as well as acquire customers for ongoing direct communication." And so on.

Then, working with the three key customer segments we'd already targeted as growth opportunities, we laid out a segment/channel grid with twelve segment/channel intersections. It was easy to spot the most important intersections—the segment of customers new to fitness would need the personal service and fit consultation that could be provided only in stores, for example—and for each priority intersection we defined the experience we wanted to deliver and laid out the ideal product selection, service level, sensory dimensions, shopping tools, and even the ideal transaction process. We also paid attention to opportunities to help customers use multiple channels for a single shopping experience. For instance, could an online shopper check and see if a local store had a desired item in stock? (Cross-channel integration of this kind was a relatively new approach at the time, and it is still not done well by many retailers.)

Finally, we drafted short stories outlining typical customer experiences that we could share throughout the organization. Through these stories, we were able to illustrate the effectiveness of consultative selling, which in turn sparked new sales training ideas for the staff training team. The stories also served as the initial scripts for vignettes we included in a video about the new brand platform and customer experience.

In the end, the framework increased marketing efficiency by helping the company target the right people in the right way. The company also determined how to get more business out of its existing channels and how to appeal to growing segments, all the while improving overall customer satisfaction.

As the number of brand touchpoints grows in today's retail environment, retailers need to focus and unify their customer experiences. A Customer Experience Architecture enables you to deliver a cohesive experience that builds your brand and your business.

Make the Small Stuff Your Business

For seventeen years in a row, Singapore Airlines (SIA) has been *Travel+Leisure* magazine's top-rated airline.[26] The airline has also consistently been one of the world's most profitable airlines, and has maintained a reputation as a trendsetter and a challenger of industry norms. "For over three decades," writers in the *Journal of Air Transport Management* observe, "SIA has managed to achieve what many others in the aviation industry can only dream of: cost-effective service excellence that is reinforced by effective human resource management and a positive company culture and image."[27]

Singapore Airlines is a great example of how a company operationalizes its brand values so thoroughly that the ethos of "sweating the small stuff" suffuses the company's business processes, the epitome of the brand-as-business philosophy. When the leaders of great brands apply their attention to detail in the running of the business, they unleash the power of their brand to focus, align, and guide every aspect of their operations.

The airline was the first to introduce hot meals, free beverages, personal entertainment systems, and video-on-demand in all cabins. Hot towels were a first, too, and they carry a unique scent. Delivering reliably on such details takes a well-trained staff, so it's no coincidence that SIA cabin and flight crews undergo some of the most rigorous training programs in the industry. Flight attendants, called "Singapore Girls," are trained for fifteen weeks, nearly twice as long as the industry average of two months.[28]

SIA expects a lot from its Singapore Girls. The company brand manual offers instructions on how to move and walk in the form-fitting flight uniforms, lists approved hairdos and foundation shades, and recommends brands and colors for lipstick and nail polish. The manual also limits Singapore Girls to wearing simple earrings and elegant watches (preferably an upscale brand). Singapore Girls in uniform are not permitted to be seen taking public transportation. Once in uniform, they must stick to taxis and limos.

As brand strategist Martin Roll puts it, the Singapore Girl embodies traditional Asian values and hospitality, which "could be described as caring, warm, gentle, elegant and serene. It is a brilliant personification of SIA's commitment to service and quality excellence." Roll points out that the Singapore Girl has achieved such iconic brand status that Madame Tussaud's Museum in London put a wax Singapore Girl on display in 1994 as the first-ever commercial figure.[29]

Emblematic of the commitment to passengers, SIA customers are treated to better, more finely appointed surroundings than the people who work in the airline's executive suite. Although the company has a world-class fleet, the company's headquarters do not feature fine decorations or furnishings. The office's simple, functional design epitomizes the company's pursuit of internal efficiency.[30]

A study of SIA in the *Journal of Air Transport Management* suggests that the company has achieved what some would consider impossible—leadership in both innovation and efficiency. The study's authors attribute this accomplishment to the implementation of "a dual strategy"—excelling in service and innovation to differentiate from competitors plus achieving cost leadership over them. The authors report that noted corporate strategy authority Michael Porter had previously deemed such a feat unachievable. He had concluded that differentiation and cost leadership were mutually exclusive because each requires a different kind of investment. Instead, SIA has defied the odds through devotion to its brand strategy.[31] As Roll puts it, "While other airlines have also pursued high service/quality brand strategies, none has been able to match Singapore Airlines in consistency, commitment, and true permeation of the brand in every facet."[32]

A lot has been written in recent years about Zappos.com and the way the company designed its entire organization around its brand values, so it's fitting to give Zappos the final word in this chapter. Zappos is famous for investing in employee training, much like REI, Chick-fil-A, and SIA. Zappos goes one step further, though, with its much-publicized policy of offering new employees a check if they leave the company after the first weeks of training.[33] That's the primary test for making sure that, although money is important to workers at the company, Zappos will keep only the employees it wants: the ones who have turned down a cash offer to *not* work there.

What may be less well known about Zappos is that it doesn't track customer call times and doesn't do commissioned sales, so caller representatives are free to spend as much time as necessary to ensure a customer is satisfied.[34] If a customer wants a product that's out of stock, the rep will research competing websites and direct the customer to them, all in the service of Zappos' Number One brand value: "Deliver WOW through service."[35]

CEO Tony Hsieh explains that in the company's early days he and his colleagues didn't intend for Zappos only to be about shoes or e-commerce. "We decided that we wanted to build our brand to be about the very best customer service and the very best customer experience. We believe that customer service shouldn't be just a department; it should be the entire company."

Making the Small Stuff Big

Like Singapore Airlines, REI, and Apple, Zappos has elevated the expression of brand through attention to detail from merely an approach to customer experience; it is the way it runs its business. Leaders of great brands may start with sweating the small stuff of package design, but they extend that discipline to *every* consumer contact with the brand. And ultimately, they focus, align, and guide every aspect of operations through the lens of the brand.

While details power great brands, they can also pose a threat. Time and attention on small matters can dilute big efforts and drain resources if they're not spent wisely. That's why sweating the small stuff must be accompanied by staying focused. Setting the right priorities and then ruthlessly sticking to them is yet another important principle great brands practice.

CHAPTER 6

Great Brands Commit and Stay Committed

One of the restaurant industry's most remarkable success stories in recent years has been that of Shake Shack, the New York–based burger-and-shake chain that began as a humble hot dog cart in 2001 and now has nearly thirty locations around the world. Out of an expressed commitment to be "the best burger company in the world," Shake Shack's CEO Randy Garutti now finds himself frequently rejecting otherwise-enviable growth opportunities, just because they somehow fail to square with the company's ambitious vision.[1]

"We get asked to cater all the time, but we fight it," Garutti told me in 2012. Catering can be a very lucrative side business for restaurants, especially for popular ones like Shake Shack where waiting lines can be long and the tables are almost always full. But Garutti determined that the Shake Shack experience is about more than the delicious food. "We want you to come to Shake Shack," he explains, pointing to the service and vibe at his locations that are as distinctive as the product's ingredients and taste. So catering isn't in Shack Shack's future, nor is the popular trend of offering convenient curbside service with a food truck.

"We had even bought the vehicle," Garutti says of the food truck concept, "but I wasn't convinced the product would be as good, and so we scrapped the idea and ate the investment."[2]

Focusing on the core of your brand—and staying committed to that focus—is the key to building a strong brand. The idea that success comes from doing a few things really well is an old one, but I've observed that the pressure to produce short-term results and the pull to imitate the successful practices of others induces many companies to lose that focus. Even well-run companies with strong brands and cultures can veer off course by mishandling their competing priorities, organizational politics, and the traditional managerial imperative to reach for top-line revenue goals.

The only defense against all these temptations and pressures is a firm commitment to setting priorities and then ruthlessly sticking to them. The leaders behind great brands drill down to their absolute aspirations—often sacrificing the sacred cows of their categories—and lock them in. Then they execute on them relentlessly so that customers over time will learn exactly what the brand stands for and come to trust that the brand will deliver.

This chapter unpacks each of these commitments, starting with setting clear priorities.

What's Your Core Ideology?

Jim Collins's research for *Built to Last* reveals that visionary companies shared an important common feature in their historical development: they all had a core ideology. "Like the fundamental ideals of a great nation, church, school, or any other enduring institution," Collins writes, "core ideology in a visionary company is a set of basic precepts that plant a fixed stake in the ground: 'This is who we are; this is what we stand for; this is what we're all about.' Like the guiding principles embodied in the American

Declaration of Independence . . . core ideology is so fundamental to the institution that it changes seldom, if ever."[3]

In Collins's view, a core ideology is "the glue that holds an organization together as it grows, decentralizes, diversifies, expands globally, and develops workplace diversity."[4] Ideally, you, your partners, and your employees should share a common core ideology, or as I call it, a brand essence, and then use these ideals as filters for decision making about emerging opportunities. But such execution is possible only when you truly commit and stay committed to those beliefs.

Great brands manage to set and keep such priorities in their decision making because their managers know how easy it is for a successful brand to lose focus. If they start out with good intentions but don't have enough of that organizational glue to guide their strategies and initiatives, they can end up going in several directions at once. No less tempting than chasing customers or following trends, the urge to grow fast often leads small, promising brands to add new services, broaden their selections, and cast a wider net to capture more sales. Steps that seem wise from a revenue standpoint can end up eroding your invaluable brand identity, even as your balance sheet grows larger and stronger in the short term.

The adage "jack of all trades, master of none" applies to many failed brands. And yet, many great brands have successfully diversified or moved beyond their original sectors. How do you grow and evolve without putting your brand at risk? Kevin Keller, author of the classic brand-building text *Strategic Brand Management*, explains that it's critical to treat your brand "with understanding and respect and a clear sense of commercial and social purpose." You must take your brand "on a well-mapped-out journey that allows the brand to profitably grow while preserving its close bonds with consumers and benefits to society as a whole."[5]

In the estimation of London business professor Constantinos C. Markides, strategic failures are commonly chalked up to "the inability to make clear, explicit choices" on three specific dimensions: target customers, offered products, and efficiency in undertaking these measures. The peril is that when large companies begin to blur their brand identities, more highly focused competitors may swoop in. Markides notes, "[O]nce formidable companies with seemingly unassailable strategic positions are humbled by relatively unknown companies that base their attacks on creating and exploiting new strategic positions."[6] The expertise demonstrated by a small, targeted brand in a single area can quickly turn the large scale and broad scope of the bigger company into a distinct competitive disadvantage, as was seen in the mid-2000s when then relatively unknown DVD-rental company Redbox spurred Blockbuster's downfall and niche green home cleaning products brand Method set market leader Clorox back on its heels.

Preserve the Core; Preserve the Business

Some companies create their own demise through opportunistic behavior. Without explicit decision making to preserve its core, an organization can get caught up in destructive market forces. But the Vanguard Group investment company shows how committing and staying committed enabled it to defy the housing bubble and remain a great brand.

For two years prior to the housing market collapse in 2009, Mabel Yu had resisted buying mortgage-backed securities for her clients at Vanguard. Yu was a fairly low-level analyst at Vanguard, but she decided she could not agree to invest client money in mortgage-backed securities that seemed far riskier to her than their AAA ratings suggested. In particular, ratings agency employees couldn't give her satisfactory explanations regarding worst-case scenarios with the proposed investments.

"I got names of the rating agency analysts, and I asked them lots of questions," Yu told National Public Radio in 2009, soon after the collapse. What began as short conversations turned into hours and hours of questioning, she recounted. She explained that in the years before the collapse, no one wanted to entertain the possibility of what actually ended up occurring—falling house prices and high unemployment leading to mortgage defaults. "If all of those things happen at same time, what would happen to our investment? I could not get a straight answer." Instead the ratings agency analysts got exasperated and told her that she worried too much. "I felt so dumb," she said.[7]

Yu's skepticism wound up saving Vanguard investors millions of dollars by avoiding what would later be regarded as Wall Street's toxic waste. And she won Vanguard's 2009 Analyst of the Year award. Her tale is retold in the book *Judgment Calls: Twelve Stories of Big Decisions and the Teams That Got Them Right.*

Author Tom Davenport writes, "Yu certainly deserves accolades, but our point is that the real hero is the organization." His interviews with company executives reveal that Yu's approach, while certainly praiseworthy, is actually typical of all Vanguard employees. Vanguard's culture, he adds, encourages dissent and independent thinking if it supports Vanguard's brand promise to invest client money wisely at the lowest possible cost.[8]

Chris Zook, author of *Repeatability: Build Enduring Businesses for a World of Constant Change*, cites Vanguard as a company that uses certain "non-negotiables" in its culture to drive strategy so dependably that the strategies seem hard-wired, or function like an operating manual. Zook told one interviewer in 2012 that, from service representatives to the CEO, the people at Vanguard use "almost identical words about the key principles that define how the company operates from a belief and loyalty to the small investor." Such top-to-bottom understanding of company strategy is missing in most organizations, said Zook. His study of data on 300,000 employee surveys showed that only about 40 percent of employees have any idea of what their companies' strategies and objectives are. "Imagine if you had a marching band or a football team where only 40 percent of the people had an idea of what the game plan was," he asked his readers to consider.[9]

Back in 2000, long before Yu had ever started at Vanguard, other analysts at the company exercised similar caution about technology stocks and avoided losing client money in the bursting Internet bubble. Vanguard CEO Bill McNabb told Tom Davenport and his coauthor, "The secret to our success is how we have managed our repeatable model to get better and better every year, while still adapting and adhering to the deep business principles that were set in place at the time of [founder] John Bogle. This discipline has not only led us in the right direction, it also often prevented us from going astray."[10] Davenport reports that when the eighty-two-year-old Bogle took Mabel Yu to a congratulatory lunch in the Vanguard cafeteria, he didn't offer to pay for her meal. Instead, he handed her the same meager $5 voucher the company gives out for birthdays. Yu responded by limiting her order to just a salad and drink. According to Yu, Davenport writes, "the whole firm is aware that one of Bogle's virtues is his frugality. Even in a decision as small as what to have for lunch, she said, 'I wanted to do things his way.'"[11]

Commitment Creates Focus

If you made a list of all the things your brand is *able to do*, you'd probably find that the list is quite long. Now try compiling another list, the list of what your brand was *made to do*. That list is probably a lot shorter.

It makes good sense to examine what your company's founders intended your company to do back when they started. What purpose did they want the company to fulfill? What did they design the organization to do well? What impact were they hoping to create? A quick audit of some of the world's most admired brands—Apple, Nordstrom, Nike, to name a few—illustrates this point quite well. All of these companies continue to do what their founders *made* them to do.

It's also clarifying to consider the timeless appeal of your brand. Amazon's CEO Jeff Bezos practices this thinking by asking, "What's not going to change over the next 10 years?" His company's commitment to three things—the best selection, the lowest prices, and the cheapest and most convenient delivery—has informed decisions that enable it to thrive while others stumble, including having enough warehouses to meet intense holiday sales demand. With a long-term view of the value that your brand delivers, he explains, you focus on "more fundamental things" than the transitory nature of competition and you develop plans that are "durable and meet important customer needs."[12]

The Krispy Kreme doughnuts brand looked a lot like a great brand in the late 1990s. The chain of doughnut shops based in the Southeast United States distinguished itself by offering a fresh, hot-doughnut experience at most of its locations (a textbook example of the five-sense experience mentioned in Chapter Five). After going public in 2000, Krispy Kreme rode a wave of growth, fueling earnings through rapid national expansion. The Krispy Kreme experience suffered as a result. In an attempt to continue fulfilling shareholders' expectations for growth, Krispy Kreme pursued new distribution points like gas stations and grocery stores, which only ended up detracting from the specialness of Krispy Kreme as a fresh, hot treat. A downward spiral took hold by 2004 as the company ended up shipping out so much product that it outpaced customer demand. Product quality suffered, sales and profits plunged, and the brand's perception was damaged almost beyond repair.[13] Only through its renewed commitment in recent years to what drove its brand success in years past has Krispy Kreme returned to profitability and regained the trust of consumers and investors alike.[14]

The Challenge of Growth

Krispy Kreme is only one extreme example of a very common phenomenon, in which growth disguises what is in fact brand cannibalization. As business professor and franchise expert Scott Shane told *CFO Magazine*, "You can often get a [retail] system to grow really large even when particular outlets aren't really profitable. . . . You might add another outlet in a market and increase your sales by 50 percent, but you might have turned franchisees in that market from profitable to unprofitable."[15] What looks like growth from the outside is actually a setup for failure.

And yet, it's a fact of life that most executives are under pressure to introduce new products and expand into new areas on a regular basis just to make their numbers and demonstrate their intent to sustain the health and valuation of the company. This is particularly true in industry categories measured on a "comparable sales versus prior year" basis, like retail and restaurants. Most of these ad hoc moves are not well aligned with the company's overall brand platform and so they tend to detract from the brand's image. In effect, they spend down the brand's equity in little ways that ultimately add up to a big deficit. In some cases, these revenue-driven moves can undermine the company's other costly brand-building initiatives by sending mixed messages and leaving customers confused. Discount promotions can have the ruinous effect of training customers to expect lower prices, which is one of the most common ways that revenue growth can weaken your brand position.

The decision to grow is often accompanied by a series of decisions to accept slightly lower levels of quality, whether it is for facilities modifications to suit different real estate requirements, ingredient changes to sign on a new distributor, or hiring standards to achieve necessary staffing levels. Each individual change seems so small and inconsequential—but when combined, the differences add up to a significant degradation of the customer experience. Sweating the small stuff gets replaced by accepting trade-offs inherent in growth.

Expanding to bring on more affiliates, franchisees, or employees means increasing the base of people who make decisions which impact the brand experience on a daily basis. This naturally leads to more inconsistencies in the delivery of that experience. Companies can try to offset this trend through rigorous training and strict policing, but a fixation on growth usually dilutes these efforts as costs are managed down. That's why Jim Collins describes core ideology as a glue that holds visionary organizations together through periods of growth and change.[16]

Great brands use their brand strategies to keep them on track because that's the only way to ensure continued relevance and resonance with customers—and continued value to shareholders. Amazon's Jeff Bezos says his company maintains the approach it started with back in 1997: "Our energy at Amazon comes from the desire to impress customers rather than the zeal to best competitors."[17] This consistency, he believes, is what produces real shareholder value. He explains, "Benjamin Graham said, 'In the short term, the stock market is a voting machine. In the long term, it's a weighing machine.' And we try to build a company that wants to be weighed and not voted upon."[18]

Setting—and keeping—priorities in a way that is consistent with your brand requires the fortitude to reject all forms of temptation to do otherwise. No doubt there were people at Shake Shack for whom the Shake Shack food truck was a beloved pet project. When Randy Garutti pulled the plug on the idea, he had to be willing to hurt some feelings and perhaps even break a few hearts among valued employees. To be great, you need to say no.

You need to be willing to play the bad guy for the greater good of the brand.

The Pitfalls of Focus

The word *focus* has come up more than a few times in this chapter. But the business world has no shortage of focus, so the true subject of discussion should be *how to direct* that focus. How, exactly, do you focus your firm's operations for maximum impact? You could choose to focus on technology, sales, distribution, or even the flavor-of-the-month business philosophy. You might reinvent your organization around a customer-centric focus. But because each of these options commits your company to a single focus that isn't grounded in your brand promise, each will likely disappoint in delivering the results you seek. Consider which one of the following areas of focus best describes your organization today.

Technology-focused organizations often operate from the inside out, starting with a new technological capability and then deciding what products to make and how to get customers to buy them. They dedicate themselves to innovation and the new products those innovations make possible. And in their first-to-market obsession, these companies usually don't employ the discipline to walk away from new technologies after yellow flags have gone up regarding feasibility, profitability, or fit with strategy. Given how difficult it is to sustain a technological advantage today, it's no wonder this type of organization eventually fails. "Innovate or die" may still work as a mantra but only if innovation serves as a means to an end—advancing the brand position—not an end unto itself.

Sales-focused organizations are those that are primarily concerned with revenue growth. These companies seek to understand their customers only to the degree that it helps them make more compelling presentations than the competitors. Salespeople will often use price concessions to make sales, undercutting the company's efforts to develop higher value perceptions that would shore up brand equity. Success is claimed when the sale is closed, with little regard to whether or not the company actually delivers the value the customer really wanted. Ultimately a sales focus fails to sustain a profitable market leadership position, and such companies fall victim to margin pressures and customer defections.

Distribution-focused organizations tend to maintain an attitude toward end users that can be summed up as "if we build it, they will come." Daily priorities at these organizations involve sustaining relationships with channel players, the people they most immediately interact with. Channel partners like value-added resellers (VARs) dominate manufacturers of computers and systems, while large retailers (Walmart and Amazon come to mind) cut profit margins for hard and soft goods manufacturers down to the bone. These distribution parties also siphon equity away from the manufacturers' brands to build up their own, and they squeeze manufacturers' margins by forcing a level playing field among competitors. Distribution-focused organizations are left with limited power in the marketplace, so they end up fighting tooth and nail for market share in existing channels instead of identifying and capturing new sources for substantive growth.

Marketing-focused organizations may appear at first glance to have the correct focus, but marketing is hardly a magic bullet. The quantity and complexity of marketing methodologies, media channels, and tools have grown exponentially in recent years, so now it is even more difficult to demystify and democratize the marketing process—at the precise time when doing so is more important than ever! For all of marketing's growing influence, the effectiveness of marketing departments can be limited by their own territorialism or organizational barriers, and the customer experience problems discussed in Chapter Five can arise if sharing information regarding customer understanding isn't valued and systematized. As the preceding chapters should have made clear, the understanding of customers, the development of value propositions, and the broad application of brand values must be aligned and integrated throughout the organization. Marketing-focused companies typically lack that integration.

Customer-focused organizations are embracing a concept that's popular now, but the customer as *the* focus of the organization runs up against the reality that it is not financially or operationally feasible for a scaled enterprise to satisfy all desires of all customers. As discussed in Chapter Four, companies that try too hard to serve all the different requirements of their user bases end up with organizational attention deficit disorder. They chase new features and benefits to offer the way dogs chase squirrels—with lots of energy and little to show for it.

Brand Focus as Your Only Focus

If none of these areas of focus are adequate, what is the solution? The conclusion must be drawn that conventional wisdom about choosing a business focus—whether it be a technology, sales, distribution, marketing, or even customer-centric approach—is an answer to the wrong question, since none of these areas of focus actually define what your company is and what your company stands for. It stands to reason that if your brand defines your company, if your brand *is* your business, then your brand is rightly the *sole focus* your organization. All these areas of focus, from technology to sales to marketing, should not be considered areas of focus at all. Instead they are merely means for executing and expressing your one true focus, your brand. When I use the expression "brand as business," this is what I mean. Brand-focused organizations may be rarities, but employing brand focus above everything else is what great brands do.

Managers of great brands know that when all the company's stakeholders share the same brand understanding, embrace the brand direction, and use a common brand platform as a filter for decision making, all their efforts remain focused and aligned. Amid vast changes in tastes, events, and trends, brands that stay true to their commitment to their core values and identity are successful in the long term. With a strong focus on the brand and its strategic platform, it is much easier to make swift, agile decisions that are consistent with all the values and attributes the company hopes to embody and deliver to its customers.

Returning once more to Shake Shack, growth there is not pursued for the sake of raising short-term revenues. Instead, growth is an option subordinate in importance to what's good for the Shake Shack brand. "We never talk in terms of 'units' or 'templates' or 'how fast can we go?'" Randy Garutti says. "We talk about, 'What great community can we be part of? How can our other restaurants get better and busier in the process of opening another Shake Shack?'" Garutti expresses the fervent belief that "the bigger we get, the smaller we have to act."[19]

Most retailers and restaurants set their course for expansion, trusting that they will identify talent to staff the new outlets as they go. Not Shake Shack. Garutti turns the question on its head and asserts that growth in organizational capabilities drives the decision to open a new location. They ask themselves, Garutti claims, "When will we have developed enough great leaders and team members who are ready to lead another Shack?" Each of those questions from Garutti represents a decision to do things a certain way, a way that contributes to defining the Shake Shack brand for its customers and for all its stakeholders. Garutti says that Shake Shack aspires to be "the 'anti-chain chain."[20] Out of that brand promise, executed across all of Shake Shack's customer touchpoints, Shake Shack has become a great brand.

◆ Tools: Five Ways to Sharpen Brand Focus

If great brands are so clear about what they stand for, how do their managers arrive at such clarity? So many great brands have powerful, charismatic leaders at the top that it's easy to assume that clarity comes from inspiration, not perspiration—but Thomas Edison was right.[21] In fact, achieving consensus in understanding what your brand stands for can be produced by any number of exercises. Some of these exercises are fun to do, even though they lead you into what amounts to fearless inquiries into the heart of what your brand is all about today—for better or worse. They're intended to shake you and your team out of your ingrained way of thinking and to reveal the full potential of your brand meaning. Here are several methods I've used with clients to help them clarify their brand essence and articulate their brands' defining values and attributes.

1. *Shoot a brand documentary.*

Task a team of employees with making a short video that attempts to capture what your brand stands for. The documentary doesn't need to have high production values. In fact, it might have greater impact and offer a sense of immediacy if it's shot quickly with an iPhone or Android phone. Describe the project along these lines:

The purpose of the video is to highlight examples of how the brand is delivered by employees and experienced by customers. Try capturing the reactions and interactions of actual customers as they experience your products or services. You might include news items or media coverage of your brand. Recap a project or company program that captures what the brand is all about. Try interviewing employees who have done something that you think exemplifies the brand. Ask employees to report on something they've seen their coworkers or strategic business partners doing that resonates with the brand platform. Once you've assembled and edited the pieces, give the documentary a title that epitomizes the content.

That title will point to your brand essence. One outdoor clothing company filmed a brand documentary that showed customers and employees using its products in extreme conditions.

The film name, *Into the Wild*, formed the basis of the brand essence: "for the love of the wild." In another case, a travel company's essence, "turning trips into journeys," was derived from the story-telling aspect of travel that was woven through all of the content in its documentary. The process of making the documentary will help clarify in everyone's mind what the brand really stands for.

2. *Write your brand's obituary.*

It's not a cheery thought, but imagine for a moment that your brand has ended its time on earth and now you need to take stock of what it was all about. It helps to think of your brand as though it were a person—the type of person the brand would be if it came to life today. Think of your brand also in terms of its totality, as all that the brand entails.

If you pretend that you are a reporter for a local newspaper who must write the obituary for this person, your brand, who just passed away today, the invented scenario can help you uncover the true nature of your brand. Once you've completed the brand obituary, your headline will reveal your brand's essence—its very reason for being—very much like the title of the documentary in the prior exercise.

Here are some questions you might seek to answer in your obituary:

- What was the brand's biggest accomplishment in life? What will it be remembered for?
- Who did the brand leave behind? What did the brand leave unaccomplished? Who will mourn or miss the brand, and why?
- What lessons can be learned from the brand's life? What can be learned from its death?
- Now that the brand is gone, who will take its place?

This obituary-writing process was particularly helpful for a struggling specialty retailer I worked with. Sales had been declining for years and the executive team had decided to reposition the brand. The problem was that no one could agree on the new direction. For the obituary process, each member of the team was assigned to write the brand's death notice and then, in a follow-up meeting, share what they wrote. In that meeting, as each obituary was read aloud, it became painfully clear how thoroughly the brand had outlived its purpose. The team members had all decided that the brand would not be missed and that it left behind no mourning fans. Quite a painful realization.

However, most of the brand obituaries also expressed fond memories of products that the company had once carried. These were useful, problem-solving products and tools that had formerly represented the company's main reason for being. The writing process helped the team recognize that their decisions to add softer, novelty-oriented products in recent years had diffused the brand's identity to the point where it had lost touch with its fans. Out of this simple writing exercise, everyone got on the same page about the need to make the brand an indispensable part of people's lives again. Ultimately we were able to articulate a new, unique essence for the brand, one that would reflect the everyday relevance of its products.

3. *Analyze your strategy via the "BARATA" framework.*

This is a very practical way to clarify the exact core of your brand, by evaluating your brand's standing according to six possible levers of brand differentiation—benefit, attribute, role, attitude, territory, awareness—which spell out "BARATA."

> *Benefit:* A tangible advantage of using your brand. ("Tide gets your clothes white.")

Attribute: A specific feature that distinguishes your brand. ("Allstate Insurance policies come with Accident Forgiveness.")

Role: The function your brand serves in customers' lives. ("Nike+ is your running partner.")

Attitude: The strong voice or point of view of your brand. (Jack In the Box's irreverent CEO character.)

Territory: The place or world invoked by the brand. (Corona beer and the beach.)

Awareness: The brand as a visual icon. (The shiny red soles of Christian Louboutin shoes.)

Go down this list to analyze which levers you and your competitors are currently using. If you find that a few levers are used by most of the brands in your category and others aren't used at all, consider how you might capture these white space points of differentiation to adopt a vantage point that will yield greater competitive advantage.

At Sony, we used the BARATA framework to develop a unique essence for the VAIO brand of computers back in the early 2000s. At the time, Dell, Compaq, and HP were the strongest PC brands, and all of them were competing on attributes (processing speeds, memory, compatibility) and benefits (responsiveness, ease of use, reliability). As a relatively new brand, VAIO was known primarily as an expensive, high-end sleekly designed laptop for CEOs and other successful business travelers. That positioning put the VAIO at a distinct disadvantage to the more established brands because it forced VAIO to compete on the basis of the same levers—attributes and benefits.

Using the BARATA framework steered us toward examining the other four levers to see which ones might prove to be more "ownable" and in sync with VAIO's strengths. We ended up aligning VAIO with going "beyond computing" as an entertainment device (the role lever) and a spirit of new creativity (the attitude lever). With role and attitude as our chief brand strategy levers, we developed a series of advertising and marketing programs that displayed the VAIO being used in new, creative ways such as digital painting, and we guided product development to provide more new experiences through the VAIO, such as watching movies on the go, which was still a novel concept in the early 2000s.

4. *Put your brand on trial.*

For thousands of years, societies have depended on courts and trials to sort out important facts that are in dispute. So why not put your brand on trial? This exercise can be one of the most revealing of all these brand essence exercises. When I led strategy development at a global advertising agency, we used this method to kick off creative brainstorming with our clients. It produces results fast, and it is usually a lot of fun to do.

You can begin by bringing in a professional mediator to serve as judge, or moderator. The jury can be recruited from consumers who are brand loyalists or, alternatively, company executives and employees can serve. Then divide your participants into two groups of five or six people. Designate one group as the prosecution and the other as the defense. The moderator then presents the defendant—the brand.

The moderator explains that the brand has been charged with the high crime of not giving its competitors a real run for their money. The defense should prepare an argument to show that the brand is a formidable competitor, while the prosecution should present the argument that the brand is just a copycat. Arguments should be based on what the brand does to differentiate itself and establish a competitive advantage. And they should rank order the evidence according to how strongly it supports their position. After each side has had the opportunity to present its case, the moderator can judge which team was more persuasive, but it's the discussion process that yields insights about the brand essence. In the heat of the teams' arguments, the unique values and attributes of the brand will become obvious, as will the points most in need of rethinking or reinforcement.

For one advertising client of mine, this exercise helped change the company executives' minds about focusing their campaign on a differentiating but potentially polarizing aspect of the brand. They had been leery of emphasizing it for fear of alienating some customers, but after putting the brand on trial and interrogating it, they realized that attribute defined the brand and deserved the spotlight.

5. *Identify your brand's archetypes.*

Film and literature present a number of universal character types, such as the Hero who overcomes great obstacles or the Jester who sees the humor in any situation. Analyzing a brand through the lens of these storytelling archetypes can help company leaders clarify the ultimate meaning and role that their brands play in customers' lives. By using consumer research, competitive analysis, and stakeholder input to identify the archetype or archetypes that best describe your brand, you can develop a clearer picture of your brand's core essence.

I once helped a household appliance business identify its brand archetype in a way that clarified its differentiation and helped its leadership team articulate the core brand values and attributes that could be applied to messaging and product design. We conducted a competitive analysis in which we audited marketing communications from the category leaders, articles that had been written about the companies, and interviews with the CEOs. It was clear from those steps that products in the category most often played the roles of the Magician and the Hero in customers' lives, with the competing brands emphasizing advanced functions and designs in its technologies. However, we believed there was greater opportunity in the market if we emphasized a more feminine personality for our brand, owing to the simplicity of the product design. So, we adopted the Innocent and the Caregiver as fresh archetypes for the brand. We used a very streamlined visual identity (lots of white space, simple typeface, minimal graphics) to convey simplicity and ease of use, and we used messaging in marketing materials that emphasized how the product line helped customers care for their homes and their families. Future product development incorporated these same values and attributes, all inspired by the unique archetypes we discovered the brand embodied.

Archetypes serve to reveal a character's purpose in a story, just as your brand archetype reveals its purpose and relevance to your customers. Take a look at ten common character archetypes below, and see which ones best clarify the role your brand plays in the story of your business and your customers' lives.

- ◆ "The Innocent" offers a simple solution to a clear problem or is associated with goodness, morality, simplicity, nostalgia, or childhood (examples: Coca-Cola, Ben & Jerry's).
- ◆ "The Regular Guy or Girl" gives people a sense of belonging and is characteristic of populist brands—those that distinguish themselves via everyday simple functionality (examples: Walmart, Wendy's).
- ◆ "The Explorer" helps people express their individuality or break with convention, characteristic of brands that present new experiences (examples: Google, Trader Joe's).
- ◆ "The Sage" serves an educational role, characteristic of brands that differentiate on the basis of quantitative information or longevity of experience (examples: NPR, IBM).

- ◆ "The Hero" solves problems, particularly difficult or socially significant ones (examples: Nike, Amazon).
- ◆ "The Outlaw" appeals to people who feel excluded or disenfranchised, representative of brands that break from category convention or compete primarily by projecting a rebellious attitude (examples: Virgin, Red Bull).
- ◆ "The Magician" offers transformative experiences, products, and services (examples: Apple, Dyson).
- ◆ "The Lover" helps people connect with others, characteristic of brands whose primary appeal is sensory and visceral (examples: Häagen-Dazs, Starbucks).
- ◆ "The Jester" helps people have a good time, representative of entertainment brands or those whose mission is to challenge established brands (examples: Geiko, HBO).
- ◆ "The Caregiver" supports families and helps people care for others, usually brands with more altruistic motives (examples: Johnson & Johnson, Volvo).

Like the other four exercises, archetypes help you identify what makes the brand's identity live and breathe. When you can conceive of your brand as though it were a person, one worthy of your respect and admiration, it will be that much easier to resist temptations to betray the brand by taking shortcuts and easy profits that risk spoiling the brand's true identity.

Once you've clarified your brand essence, you should combine it with your Competitive Brand Positioning, as discussed in Chapter Four, to construct your brand platform. Your brand essence articulates what your brand stands for; your Competitive Brand Positioning explains how you compete against other brands. Your brand platform, therefore, expresses the strategic underpinnings of your business and can be used a framework for implementing the brand-as-business approach.

Sacrificing the Sacred to Define Your Brand

A recurring theme in this chapter is the necessity of sacrifice in creating and sustaining a great brand. Great brands sacrifice even the most sacred cows—short-term profit and growth—in their categories because that's often the most effective way to differentiate. If you set different day-to-day priorities from your competitors, you can't help but stand out. Great brands defy conventional wisdom in order to preserve their defining values and attributes. They favor building long-term brand image, maintaining trust with existing customers, and adhering to set strategies that target best prospects.

Southwest Airlines is the best-known example of a company that has always defied conventional wisdom in order to preserve its defining values and attributes. Southwest's founders challenged category conventions from the start by occupying the difficult market niche of short-haul flights and skipping typical sources of airline profitability such as premium-class seating. The airline has consistently performed as one of the most profitable in its industry, and its sacrifices, once derided as serious obstacles to the company's long-term viability, are now credited with fueling the company's success.[22]

Southwest's sacrifices exemplify the strategy of a challenger brand. As noted in Chapter Four, challenger brands (described by Adam Morgan in his book, *Eating the Big Fish*) develop clarity of their brand identity and project it with precision and strength. A challenger brand (defined by Morgan as a "number-two or number-three brand who is up against a much bigger and more muscular brand leader—the Establishment Brand") also often uses sacrifice to unseat market leaders.[23] Think Avis, whose "We're number two, so we try harder" theme line most overtly articulated the challenger ideal, and Virgin, which selects businesses to enter based on the identification of entrenched category leaders that need to be taken down.

Morgan describes the very distinctive kinds of sacrifices challenger brands make:

Target sacrifices (choosing customer loyalty over customer quantity): Fox Network's early 1990s groundbreaking programming (*The Simpsons, The X-Files*) took the risk of turning off many older, more conservative viewers. But by sacrificing mainstream appeal, Fox was rewarded with clear differentiation from the established players, and with two kinds of loyalty—both viewership and viewer attention—among eighteen-to-thirty-four-year-olds, among the most fickle of audiences.[24] Sacrifice is how Fox became the fourth network.

Reach sacrifices (favoring exclusivity over broad awareness): This category can also be called "frequency sacrifice." The decision by Absolut Vodka's brand managers to consistently advertise on the back covers of magazines was limiting—paying a significant premium for the position meant they could afford fewer placements. But doing so gave the brand visibility and a sense of exclusivity from all the other print advertisers and reinforced the air of prestige that Absolut has cultivated since its beginning.[25]

Distribution sacrifices (ensuring desirability over availability): Oakley used to insist on brand discoverability and authenticity. So it restricted its product distribution to only those sporting outlets that it believed represented opinion leadership in its categories, such as the most hard-core bike shop in each city. By first selling exclusively to opinion leaders, Oakley created credibility and demand in the mainstream market, a foundation that served the brand well when it came time to expand.[26] More recently Lululemon Athletica has succeeded with a similar strategy, as discussed in Chapter Four.

Sacrifice may not always be a part of the strategic plan, but when sacrifices are called for by great brands, they proceed from the company's committed priorities. In 1982, after seven people in Chicago died of poisoning after taking extra strength Tylenol, parent company Johnson & Johnson halted all advertising and removed all 31 million Tylenol bottles from store shelves at a cost of $100 million. It had been clear almost from the start that someone had tampered with Tylenol in the stores, not in J&J's manufacturing plants. J&J executives could have taken the position that the deaths weren't the company's fault. But instead the company followed the first sentence of its company credo of putting the well-being of its customers first, above all other considerations including loss of sales.[27] The company chair was hailed at the time for his leadership in ordering a complete recall and for his forthrightness with the press.[28]

The Tylenol story isn't just a lesson in effective crisis communication—it's a demonstration of a company making sacrifices and following its values despite some very negative potential outcomes. J&J took responsibility for the crisis and removed all of its product from the shelf at great cost because it took its credo seriously, as a guide for setting priorities and making sacrifices. As a result, it set a new high standard for corporate behavior when brands are damaged by negative news.

"Before 1982, nobody ever recalled anything," a Johnson & Johnson's public relations adviser told the *New York Times* in 2002. "Companies often fiddle while Rome burns." And yet, the *Times* noted that Johnson & Johnson's stock price returned to its previous high within two months of the crisis and that Tylenol's market share had recovered almost completely within a year. The headline for the article was "Tylenol Made a Hero of Johnson & Johnson."[29]

Committing for the Long Term

Sacrifices rarely pay off in the short term. To realize the brand-building benefit of sticking to your priorities despite the sacrifices, you need to lock them in for the long term.

Above all, the managers of great brands make long-term commitments. They know that when you commit to your brand identity internally and sear it into your customers' minds clearly and consistently, the value proposition and points of difference of your brand become unmistakable and unforgettable. So they put their brands in the driver's seat of their organizations and rely on them to navigate uncertain circumstances and difficult decisions.

This is the fanatical adherence to the company's vision that Jim Collins advocates in *Good to Great: Why Some Companies Make the Leap . . . and Others Don't*. "A great company is much more likely to die of indigestion from too much opportunity than starvation from too little," Collins writes. "The challenge becomes not opportunity creation, but opportunity selection. It takes discipline to say 'No, thank you' to big opportunities. The fact that something is a 'once-in-a-lifetime' opportunity is irrelevant."[30]

Long-term commitments are often that simple, like J&J's commitment to customer well-being and Vanguard's commitment to the wisest investments at the lowest cost. At the Container Store, chairman and chief executive officer Kip Tindell takes pride in the way his company has dispensed with phone-book-sized procedural manuals and instead relies on a set of seven principles to keep employees "on track, focused and fulfilled."[31]

Commitment Facilitates Flexibility

To some, the idea of such long-term commitments might seem confining. How do you stay flexible if you're locked in to one long-term way of thinking? Tindell sees it the other way around. The payoff from a long-term commitment to the Container Store's principles, from Tindell's perspective, is *greater* flexibility for everyone who signs on to the principles.

"We don't believe in big, thick rule books, because they tie people up in knots," he told *Fast Company* back in 2002. So the company remains flexible and uses the Foundation Principles to "make it easier for us to operate as a team—as opposed to 2,000 yahoos going off in 2,000 different directions."[32]

The Container Store's story shows how growth and commitment can go hand in hand in building a brand. The Dallas-based company, founded in 1978, grew slowly in its first decade and then suddenly had more success than it could handle with the opening of its Houston store in 1988. Sales were three to four times higher than anything management had ever seen before, and in an attempt to keep up, the company hired more new people quickly, just to get more bodies in the store. Customer service, company culture, and leadership at the store were all suffering as a result.[33]

Tindell in desperation called a meeting of the employees at the store manager's house. To prepare for what he was going to say, he sorted through a personal file folder of inspirational thoughts he'd been collecting since high school. Out of about a hundred scraps of paper in his "Philosophy Epistle" folder, Tindell picked out a handful that he thought reflected what the company was already doing when it was at its best. "We thought this, we thought that, but it had never been written down before," he recalled in 2010. At the meeting, he was a little afraid what he had to say would be considered corny, but the opposite happened. Outlining what the company believed in and how it stays committed to the principles created "incredible fierce pride."[34] The foundation principles—including "1 Great Person = 3 Good People" and "Communication IS Leadership"—have since been widely distributed throughout the organization.

The Container Store principles make everyone in the company sure of what the company is committed to in the long term. Even though the company has far fewer employee rules and gives its employees lots of latitude in dealing with customers, the company's long-term commitment to its principles ensures that customers get a distinctive experience at the Container Store that makes visits there unforgettable. In Tindell's words, "We all agree on the ends . . . as a result, we have people unshackled to choose any means to those ends, but it's not mayhem because our foundation principles kind of tie us together."[35]

How has it all worked? Company sales passed $700 million in 2012, a huge jump from 2011's sales of $633 million.[36] Those who have tried to steal market share from the Container Store by using the traditional retail strategy of cutting costs and lowering prices have not fared well. The last of the Container Store's big competitors shut its doors in 2006.

Great Brands Persevere

By its very nature, commitment to a brand platform requires a brand that continues to deliver value over the long term. Brands therefore must be sustainable and integral—sustainable in the sense that their relevance is evergreen, and integral in the sense that they create value for everyone involved in their businesses.

From seeking emotional connections to advancing cultural movements to attracting like-minded customers to sweating the small stuff, this book has explained how great brands achieve sustainable relevance. The next step is to create shared value through business design and execution.

CHAPTER 7

Great Brands Never Have to "Give Back"

On November 25, 2012, the outdoor clothing retailer Patagonia ran one of the most unusual Black Friday ads in the history of the *New York Times*. Above an image of one of the company's most popular products, the full-page ad declared in large, bold lettering: "DON'T BUY THIS JACKET." The text below explained that the holiday season was a good time to consider the environmental impact of modern consumerism. "Because Patagonia wants to be in business for a good long time," the ad read, "and leave a world inhabitable for our kids—we want to do the opposite of every other business today. We ask you to buy less and to reflect before you spend a dime on this jacket or anything else."[1]

At the same time, Patagonia launched what it calls the "Common Threads Initiative," in which the company promises to repair damaged Patagonia products and help owners resell their used Patagonia products on a special eBay page. The initiative also encourages Patagonia customers to take a pledge committing themselves to buy only long-lasting goods, repair the goods when they break, and resell, give away, or recycle products when they're no longer needed.[2]

"It is not a marketing shtick," Vickie Achee, Patagonia's head of marketing for North America retail, explained to me. "It is not a new program to get more customers or get more revenue. It really is how we live, as [Patagonia] employees. This is just another extension of what we really do, and encouraging our customers to join us."[3] A version of the ad, with the Common Threads pledge, went out to thousands of Patagonia e-mail subscribers on the Monday following Black Friday, "Cyber Monday," which to retailers is fast becoming as important of a sales day as Black Friday.[4]

Patagonia, like many great brands, has cultivated a unique corporate culture that frequently pushes it to the forefront of various social and cultural movements. In fact, driving positive social change is one of the most distinguishing marks of great brands—even though great brands often don't engage in typical corporate social responsibility (CSR) activities like making attention-getting donations or sponsoring the usual organizations. Instead, their people design and run their businesses to make a significant, sustainable positive impact on society.

Great brands have no need to "give back" to society in the form of charitable contributions because they employ a more integrated approach, as they do in all aspects of their businesses. They don't simply take a few visible actions that create a positive impression with customers. They redefine CSR itself as *CSV*, creating shared value for their customers, employees, business alliances, investors, and communities, by establishing relevance in increasingly vital and pervasive areas. I've developed a framework called Level 5 Relevance to guide this approach.

As a result, great brands are themselves becoming a force for positive social change, rather than simply supporting external programs. They have designed their businesses or are innovating new business processes to create value for themselves and others through the inner workings of their operations. Some have reconceived their products to address social issues; others have transformed their supply chains and operating procedures. What all these great brands have in common is the application of the brand-as-business approach to bettering the world.

The End of "Goodwashing"

The media had a field day with Mark Zuckerberg in September, 2010. After *Forbes* revealed that the Facebook founder and CEO had climbed to the thirty-fifth position on its annual list of wealthy Americans—and the movie *The Social Network*, with its rather unfavorable portrayal of Zuckerberg, was scheduled to launch—commentators swooped in to critique another announcement: Zuckerberg would be donating $100 million to help fix schools in Newark, New Jersey.[5] This was a gift many times larger than the school system—one of the country's worst at the time—had ever received. Coverage of the news focused on the dubious timing of the announcement and called the donation a calculated move. Media outlets went to work sussing out whether or not it was intended as a public relations coup.

Unfortunately a more significant failing of Zuckerberg's donation wasn't given the same scrutiny. When viewed through the lens of brand integrity, it's clear that the gift was lacking. There was no tie-in to Facebook, its values, or its employees, nor to Zuckerberg's own personal brand as a hacker. The donation was as irrelevant to Zuckerberg and his company as was Danica Patrick's appearance in GoDaddy.com TV commercials during the Super Bowl. There was no formal initiative to harness Facebook's considerable brainpower to transform the education process or put Facebook's resources and know-how to work on its behalf.[6]

Contrast that with the efforts of AT&T, which has a planned investment of up to $350 million in its high school "Aspire" program, launched in 2008. As of 2013, AT&T employees had contributed 270,000 hours to a program that offers high schoolers the opportunity to shadow AT&T employees and get an invaluable glimpse of the real world of work through mentoring, internships, and other voluntary programs. The company is taking what it calls a "socially innovative" approach to the lack of college- and workplace-readiness among teenagers at risk for dropping out of high school. It's going beyond traditional philanthropy—which typically involves only charitable giving—and is directing its capabilities and resources to address social issues critical to the company's future. The connection between a workforce that's better prepared to meet global competition and AT&T's long-term viability is clear, and the active engagement of AT&T employees is integral to the effort. And, of course Aspire employs AT&T's technology and the company's internal start-up incubator, AT&T Foundry, so it advances AT&T's brand equity in innovation.[7]

A More Integrated Approach

AT&T is only one of many companies awakening to the realization that it takes more than large attention-getting gestures to be truly socially responsible. Consumers have begun demanding a more integrated approach. They want companies to stop doing a few virtuous things to bolster their reputations ("goodwashing"), and instead start using the power of their brands to inspire real change and have an overall beneficial impact on society.

Over ten years of research by MORI, an international research firm, has shown CSR becoming increasingly prominent. MORI reports that the factors that used to matter most to consumers when forming an opinion of a company were product quality, value for money, and financial performance. Now, the most commonly mentioned factors relate to corporate responsibility—treatment of employees, community involvement, and ethical and environmental issues.[8]

Consumers have come to realize that society and business can and should be integrated. According to the Edelman public relations firm, a full 76 percent of consumers in 2012 said they believe it is acceptable for brands to support good causes and make money at the same time—up from 33 percent in 2008. Eighty-seven percent of consumers believe business should place at least equal emphasis on social interests and on business interests.[9]

News reports of scandals over crooked accounting methods, environmental destruction, excessive executive compensation, and complaints of sexual harassment have skyrocketed in the last ten years, putting business ethics on consumers' radar screens like never before. Coupled with the growing belief that profits and social progress should not be mutually exclusive goals, increasing numbers of people are saying they will do business only with respectable companies.

MORI reports the percentage of people saying corporate responsibility is very important in their purchasing decisions has doubled in just the past five years.[10] According to Edelman's research, 73 percent say they would switch brands if a similar brand supported a good cause, and similar numbers say they would recommend and promote those brands to others. Just four years ago, Edelman found that only 52 percent said they'd recommend a cause-related brand.[11]

Doing well by doing good is not a new idea. But the integrity with which it should be pursued is. An influential article published in 2012 by John Gerzema and David Roth cautions that we are entering a new era where corporate reputation and brand management are one and the same.[12]

The article points to an integrated four-point model of reputation made up of success, fairness, responsibility, and trust. The four components are defined this way:

- Success: Innovative, associated with quality products, and financially strong.
- Fairness: Well priced, offering good value for money, honest and decent in relationships with customers, suppliers, and other companies.
- Responsibility: Respectful of employees, scrupulous about supply chain practices, and protective of the environment.
- Trust: Consistently delivers on promises about products and services.[13]

According to Gerzema and Roth, until recently these four components were not commonly well integrated. The hard and practical business considerations of success and fairness drove the business while the soft considerations of responsibility and trust formed a protective moat around them. But, the article cautions, "Success today requires integrating these components into all levels of the business. This approach produces brand integrity, a tensile internal strength that's much more durable than the 'moat.' It is vitally important for companies to understand that they have two types of shareholders, those who hold stocks and those who buy products and services."[14] The point is that society's demands for transparency and participation have drained the moat. Success and fairness both must be executed with responsibility and trust in mind, every step of the way.

It's the dawning of a new age of CSR.

Rethinking CSR

Great brands are ushering in this new age by aligning their social efforts with their business strategies and operations, thereby enhancing their customer appeal and long-term competitiveness. Starbucks' "Create Jobs for USA" program, for example, provides financing to undercapitalized community businesses, weaving together the company's socially oriented culture and its business goals. "When businesses use their resources and scale for good, they can make a positive difference in the communities they serve," CEO Howard Schultz said in a statement issued in 2012. "It is this philosophy that continues to inspire Starbucks to consider how other business decisions we make can reap benefits for and beyond our partners, customers and shareholders."[15]

The program is an authentic expression of the company's reliance on the communities it does business in, its emotional connection with customers, and its mission to inspire and nurture the human spirit. It really is a case where the company's good and the public good are aligned. As such, it does more for Starbucks' brand image, more for its bottom line, and more for the actual success of the social enterprise than any other more typical "giving back" effort.

The term "giving back" has achieved such widespread cultural currency that it's easy to forget the negative connotation it implies. Giving back suggests that you've taken something that needs to be paid back to balance out your karma, that you've diminished society in some way and as an act of contrition you're making up for the transgression. But because great brands manage to make profits while creating value for *all* their stakeholders, they don't need to give back anything. They are no longer in the business of taking with one hand and giving back with the other.

In the wise words of London-based brand strategy consultant Guy Champniss, real traction in CSR and sustainability comes from recognizing "it's no longer about refining your brand value proposition (to be sold). It's about discovering your brand value principles (to be shared). If we get this right, the brand is unleashed as a value driver, and sustainability will finally have the opportunity to emerge as a charismatic natural outcome."[16] This takes to an even higher level the earlier observation that the integration of reputation and brand management means that the creation of social value and business value become one and the same.

From CSR to CSV

In my work with Fortune 1000 companies representing a wide range of industries, I see business leaders trying to meet their social responsibilities in ways that are clearly not satisfying to them or their people. Some respond passively to charitable solicitations and feel as though they're being used as a kind of corporate Santa Claus. Others cherry-pick a few causes and worry if they are somehow disappointing or alienating the sponsors of other worthy causes. Still others commit deeply to pet causes that affect them personally, without considering whether these pet causes are aligned with the goals of their respective companies. In each of these approaches, the possibilities of building their brands and growing their businesses through social initiatives remain overlooked.

The leaders of great brands take a distinctly different approach. They consider their opportunities more holistically. Rosabeth Moss Kanter, author of *The Vanguard Corporation*, calls their approach "bringing society in." It's a different way of thinking, she explains. Bringing society in prompts people to say, "We have a purpose beyond today's markets and products, and we should think about that. How is society changing? What are the big problem areas? What are our capabilities so that maybe we can find a commercial opportunity that also does good?"[17]

This enlightened approach enables great brands to create value that can be shared among internal stakeholders (executives, employees, and investors) and external ones, which include suppliers, agencies, strategic partners, industry influencers, local communities, and finally, customers. Kanter notes that companies gain the internal benefits of innovation and motivation, as well as external public support, if they adopt this shared value approach—and they don't struggle with "being coherent and finding business opportunities."[18] The managers of great brands, therefore, replace CSR with *CSV*—creating shared value.

What CSV entails becomes clear through further examination of Patagonia. The Patagonia brand is all about courage, commitment, and challenging conventions—in everything it does. In his book, *Let My People Go Surfing*, founder Yvon Chouinard explains, "The first part of our mission statement, 'Make the best product' is the raison d'être of Patagonia and the cornerstone of our business philosophy. We are a product-driven company, and without a tangible product there would obviously be no business and the other goals of our mission statement would thus be irrelevant. Having quality, useful products anchors our business in the real world and allows us to expand our mission."[19]

Yet the company mission speaks to more than product excellence. It also includes "causing no unnecessary harm" and "using business to inspire and implement solutions to the environmental crisis."[20] To these ends, Patagonia developed "The Footprint Chronicles," an online resource that offers documentation on every product the company makes, where it came from, and how it was made, starting with the raw materials.[21]

To outsiders, the program gives access to a reporting mechanism on the company's progress in fulfilling its mission, and to those who work at Patagonia, it provides focus and a clear goal since the company has made a commitment and a corporate priority to align its supply chain with its values. Attention to The Footprint Chronicles reduces the company's impact on the environment. It helps develop a more sustainable supply chain and increase production efficiencies that benefit the company and shareholders, and it engages consumers in transparent communication that wins their trust and loyalty. It forms an ideal win-win-win-win approach because of its widespread value creation.

Creating shared value involves establishing relevance in a diverse and increasingly resonant set of areas. When viewed through the lens of ability to increase brand resonance with multiple stakeholder groups, social initiatives are seen not as an obligation (something you need to do because it's expected) but as an opportunity (something you want to do, because it can benefit everyone, including your shareholders). The goal and decision filter about how to reach that goal shifts accordingly, from one of responsibility (something to be done and checked off a list) to one of relevance (something to seek to achieve and continuously sustain). It's easy to see how prospects for brand and business growth are much greater in pursuing opportunities and increasing relevance than in fulfilling obligations and responsibilities.

◆ *Tool:* Creating Shared Value with the Level 5 Relevance Framework

To identify how your organization can embrace and execute on an effective social strategy, consider how you might achieve five levels of social relevance: industry, community, target, brand positioning, and values. Each of these is a level in the Level 5 Relevance framework I've crafted; progressing through each will allow you to create shared value across your enterprise. Each level in the framework establishes important meaning and represents a step in the path to achieving relevance of the highest order.

Here are examples of each level as they appear when the Level 5 Relevance framework is applied to the restaurant industry:

1. *Industry Relevance*—industry association campaign: Your company should get involved with causes that align with your industry; for restaurants, fighting childhood obesity through

the National Restaurant Association's Kids Live Well campaign is a natural fit. Financial support is a good first step, but it shouldn't be your only one. Engage your people, systems, network, and other resources with these industry efforts to make a more integral and differentiated impact.

2. *Community Relevance*—disaster relief efforts: Captain D's Seafood Kitchen's Mobile Kitchen rolled into Tuscaloosa, Alabama, after a hurricane hit the area in 2011, and by feeding relief workers and residents, it served a critical role in meeting the needs of its local community.[22]

3. *Target Relevance*—the Ronald McDonald House Charities: Through this long-standing effort, McDonald's shares its commitment to improving the health and well-being of children with its primary customer target segment, families.

4. *Brand Positioning Relevance*—Chipotle's Veggie U program: Chipotle Mexican Grill advances its "Food with Integrity" brand platform by helping nonprofits like Veggie U, which gives students the opportunity to experience the process of planting, growing, and harvesting fresh produce.[23]

5. *Values Relevance*—Shake Shack's Stand for Something Good initiatives: Hospitality is one defining value of Shake Shack, the New York–based burger-and-shake chain I describe in Chapter Six. So the company has teamed up with the Hearing Access Program to install audio induction loops in its locations to ensure that its bustling restaurants are welcoming to customers who are hard of hearing.[24]

Together, these five levels of relevance give you a framework to explore and engage the societal and cultural resonance of your brand to benefit all of your stakeholders. They provide a more positive and fruitful motivation than a bunch of random requests to respond to or a list of responsibilities to fulfill. So use this Level 5 Relevance framework as a guide on your journey from responsibility to relevance, and as a hierarchy to categorize and map the progression of your various efforts.

It may not be possible to establish relevance at every level, but each is a piece that contributes to a sum that is greater than the parts because relevance in one area usually contributes to greater relevance in others. For example, the community and the target audience of a business often overlap, particularly for retail companies, so an effort designed to speak to the community may also enhance the brand's importance to its target. Brand positioning often draws on the competitive advantage that certain corporate values produce, so a single social program may easily achieve relevance on both the brand positioning and values levels.

Also, the levels of relevance may be pursued and achieved in a different order, but conceiving them as an upward progression of significance reflects how increasingly vital and pervasive each area is in the ecosystem of your stakeholders and points you to the ultimate goal of values relevance. When your social efforts speak to values—tenets such as generosity, individual expression, or stewardship that are embraced by people and organizations and help society prosper and thrive—your brand creates value that is far broader, deeper, and longer-lasting than your commercial footprint.

There is one important caveat in all of this value creation: it can't be disconnected from your day-to-day business. Creating shared value is as much about using fair pricing, treating people with respect, employing ethical business practices, and selling great products as it is about impact on society and creation of positive change. If Patagonia's products fall apart or if Shake Shack's employees are rude, no amount of awe-inspiring social initiatives will compel customers to the brand. "People are telling us that corporate responsibility begins with helping 'me,' the individual consumer, before it expands outward into CSR-like initiatives," says Anne Bahr Thompson, founder of Onesixtyfourth and CultureQ research. "For it to be meaningful, corporate citizenship should first integrate the values that are important to people in their daily lives. After that is done, a corporation should connect people to something bigger than themselves—their communities, their country, people across the world, and the planet."[25]

As you pursue greater levels of relevance, you end up doing what great brands do. You design and develop your business so that socially responsible practices are embedded into your core, aligned and integrated with each other, and make you valuable to all your stakeholders.

Making the Move to Level 5 Relevance

Getting to Level 5 Relevance requires a series of deliberate steps. The evolution from CSR to CSV is best illustrated through the growth of Firehouse Subs since its founding in 1994. The fast-casual sandwich chain was started by a pair of brothers who hail from a family with more than two hundred combined years of firefighting service in its history. And yet, in its early years, before the founders decided their charitable efforts would be best directed at a cause or mission closely related to the company's firefighting heritage, Firehouse Subs was involved a variety of charities with little relevance to its brand. In 2005, it created the Public Safety Foundation and began donating lifesaving equipment and providing disaster assistance and educational opportunities in addition to funds to public safety groups such as fire departments, EMS units, and police departments.[26]

Level 5 Relevance starts with leaders leading, as those at Firehouse Subs did: they put a stake in the ground and committed to making their values more than words on a break room plaque. You too will need to incorporate your social priorities into your strategic plan and allocate resources in terms of people, funding, and your own time and attention if you want to give them real traction.

Taking this first step requires you to examine your business and ask some probing questions to operationalize your vision. Consider your business model—do you perhaps simply need to enhance your existing business? Or maybe you need to reimagine your model? Or invent an entirely new business? Designing holistic, human-centered systems that deliver real value requires you to address some difficult questions: What comprises your market ecosystem? Who are your most important stakeholders? What goals do you share? What is the value you really create and how do you create it? Which business activities are critical for you to engage in? Which are discretionary or distracting? Do your business outputs (products and revenues) justify the inputs (assets, relationships, resources)? What resources are you exploiting or wasting? What problems are by-products of the way you do business? The Public Safety Foundation was a logical conclusion when the Firehouse Subs leaders asked themselves these questions.

The next step in pursuit of Level 5 Relevance involves engaging your employees. The importance of internal alignment and engagement here is related to the importance of culture building discussed in Chapter One. Instead of rushing to issue press releases to promote your social activities, starting inside your company ensures those activities have the traction to warrant such fanfare. Firehouse Subs' CEO Don Fox says that when he and his leadership team took the time to help employees at restaurants engage with the Public Safety Foundation program, customers' donations at those restaurants increased over 50 percent. Managers led "crew rallies" in which they educated employees throughout the chain on the origin and mission of the foundation, sharing real-life stories about people who have benefited from its work. The objective was to raise awareness, sensitize and engage staff with the mission, and help them understand what role they could play in fostering its success. After all, the leadership team concluded, if our people aren't clear on where we're going and how we're going to get there, how will those outside our organization get it?[27]

Just as brand culture building extends to external stakeholders, Level 5 Relevance should as well. With employees engaged, turn your attention to mobilizing your other stakeholders. This step might mean, for example, collaborating with suppliers to develop different sourcing methods or getting your financing partners to support the new investments you need to make.

For Firehouse, the key external stakeholders are its franchisees and the local communities where its shops are located. For franchisees, commitment to the foundation serves as a critical screening criterion—and the company places the majority of responsibility for engaging employees and customers in the foundation on the franchisees' shoulders.[28] To engage its local communities, the company began several initiatives, including its "Hero Cups" program, in which a local citizen's lifesaving efforts are honored with a special collector soda cup featuring the honoree's picture and a brief story about the heroic act.[29]

With your employees and other stakeholders on board, you can create a compelling narrative to communicate your vision—and you should continue to tell your story, adding examples of actions and outcomes as you make progress. The Public Safety Foundation has grown into a prominent and integrated part of the Firehouse Subs story as captured on the company's website: "Featuring second-to-none sub sandwiches, and a commitment to the communities they serve, Firehouse Subs is a daily affirmation that serving good food and doing good belong together."[30] Stories and messaging about fundraising and outcomes are woven into the company's social media narrative. One picturesque example is the Pickle Bucket photo contest (proceeds from Pickle Bucket purchases are donated to the foundation).[31]

CEO Don Fox and other leaders who have undertaken similar business redesigns have learned some lessons along their Level 5 Relevance journey. They've found you are most likely to succeed if you:

Pursue a combination of efforts. A single program is not likely to achieve all five levels, so it's best to develop a portfolio of related activities and initiatives that together fulfill your objectives.

Don't spread your efforts too thin. As with all aspects of brand-building, it's better to do a few things well than a lot of things halfway. Focus your efforts and make sure you allocate the resources they need to succeed.

Make the long-term commitment. Level 5 Relevance can't be rushed. You need time to adapt your systems, not to mention your thinking. And it will take customers awhile before they notice your efforts. Then they'll wait to see whether or not you're really committed before they support you.

Don't go it alone. Many of the most successful efforts rely on strong partnerships with like-minded organizations. Even consider partnering with others in your category. Unlike market share, social efforts aren't a zero sum game.

Relevance Produces Results

The journey to Level 5 Relevance is an upward spiral of activity that can propel your business to new heights. Across the board in 2012, sales at Firehouse Subs increased 35 percent while it opened nearly a hundred new stores.[32] The founders credit the Public Safety Foundation with giving substance and credibility to the Firehouse brand as it is introduced to new markets. It's a vehicle to leverage its firefighting theme as a differentiator in a category crowded by fast-growing brands like Subway and Quizno's.[33]

As Firehouse's foundation gains traction, the company has begun to extend its donations and support to a larger audience including municipal and volunteer fire departments, police departments, and emergency medical services to volunteer organizations like the American Red Cross, and to public school systems. This increases its brand awareness and expands its brand equity.[34]

CEO Don Fox credits the foundation with playing a critical role in creating an employee experience that is as formative as possible. And—in 2012 and for the third consecutive year—Firehouse validated the correlation between franchisee engagement with the Public Safety Foundation and higher customer ratings for "Social Responsibility" and "Supporting Local Community Activities."

Perhaps the most tangible result of the company's efforts is seen in the difference in sales performance between the Firehouse Subs locations that actively participate in the foundation and those that don't. Restaurants in the top quarter of donation amounts generated significantly higher sales performance (27.8 percent higher sales for the most engaged franchisees over the least engaged).[35]

Stronger sales performance isn't the only financial benefit enjoyed by socially conscious companies like Firehouse Subs. Social impact strategies have been proven to increase corporate leverage. According to research conducted by the Harvard and London Business Schools, social relevance encourages transparency, which in turn builds good will, easing the fears of investors—whose confidence shows up on the balance sheet. The report also states that firms with better social performance records are more likely to exercise overall transparency in their corporate cultures, and therefore enjoy greater access to capital.[36] In addition, securities analysts have become more likely to recommend a stock buy for socially responsible firms, report another pair of Harvard and London Business Schools professors.[37]

There's a growing awareness in investing circles that socially sustainable companies tend to be economically sustainable. Chamath Palihapitiya, a multimillionaire and former Facebook executive, has founded the Social+Capital Partnership venture fund on the principle that companies helping people address difficult social problems are likely to be lucrative investment opportunities.[38]

A 2012 *BusinessWeek* profile of Palihapitiya describes him as excited about investing in socially beneficial advances such as an inexpensive microchip that can do simple and fast blood analysis, a mobile phone app that treats anxiety through automated exercises, and a free online university for low-income teenagers around the world. "If you focus on impact and think about generating impact, you will make money," Palihapitiya says. His goal is to create a new model of what he calls "activist capitalism."[39]

The idea that a socially oriented business can produce both social good and profits is one that the folks at Patagonia aren't shy about expressing either. Patagonia founder Yvon Chouinard once told *Grist* magazine, "Every time I made the decision because it was the right thing to do, I've ended up making actually more money."[40] Rose Marcario, Patagonia's current CEO, attributes the sales growth the company experienced in 2012 to shoppers embracing its values, saying, "Even though it was a really horrible time during the recession, a lot of consumers were really drawn to Patagonia's brand because they believe in the ethos."[41]

Starting with the End in Mind

A new breed of start-up company is embracing social relevance as a part of their DNA and business plan, from day one. These are companies that have no problem reconciling doing good with doing well because they've designed their business model on the total interdependence between the two concepts in whatever they do.

The mission of U.K. smoothie-maker Innocent Drinks is to become "The Earth's favourite little food company."[42] Company founder Richard Reed says that's a vision that "encapsulates both the scale of ambition and the fact that our business has to be done in conjunction with Mother Nature, not at her expense. We also want to prove that there is profit in ethics and that business can, and must, be a source of positive change in society."[43]

With such an ambitious purpose to fulfill, Innocent Drinks makes the promise—and prints it clearly on its bottles—that its products contain only fresh fruit, with no preservatives. Each bottle also offers the recommended daily allowance for at least two kinds of fruit. The company tries to source as much fruit as it can from Europe, and works with Rainforest Alliance to ensure that fruit from far overseas was grown sustainably. Similar to Patagonia, Innocent Drinks works deep within its supply chain to ensure that manufacturing sites recycle and raise their rates of energy efficiency and water conservation.[44]

Ecomagining the Future

Skeptics are right, nonetheless, to wonder how well the approach can work for companies without the niche brand status that Innocent and Patagonia enjoy, or ones that didn't start with a social purpose. The GE Ecomagination initiative is especially interesting in that context, as it is one of the boldest attempts by any major company to drive corporate growth directly through a social strategy.

"When [our customers] win, GE wins," CEO Jeffrey Immelt said when he launched the company's Ecomagination program in 2005, drawing a very direct connection between doing good and doing well. "Our customers deal with some of society's toughest environmental and sustainability challenges. Ecomagination will produce products that help customers find the right solutions to these issues. That's good for the environment and good for business."[45]

Ecomagination represents GE's commitment to make profits by making a better world. In seeking innovative solutions for reducing air pollution, increasing energy efficiency, and conserving water, the company is pursuing a range of programs and technologies which create value for customers, employees, investors, and the planet.

Ultimately Ecomagination is a growth strategy for the company, Lorraine Bolsinger (GE's vice president in charge of Ecomagination), told CNET.com in 2007. "It's pretty easy to understand why we would have been in the space so early on. You might say we are really smart, we're really progressive, and I'd like to think that. It's also because of the very nature of things that we make."[46]

In 2010, GE announced the "Ecomagination Challenge," a unique open call to businesses, entrepreneurs, innovators, and students for the best ideas in creating, connecting, and using power.[47] It set out to find and fund promising technologies, and submissions came in from 1,600 companies hailing from more than 150 countries. The viable business ideas ranged from highly advanced water meters to de-icing wind turbines, and within the year GE wound up committing $134 million in twenty-two investments and partnerships.[48] Another $1.1 million was dispensed in the form of innovation awards and seed funding for start-up companies. Another product of that effort—a significant departure from GE's normal management-led way of doing things—was a total of seventy-four thousand registered online visitors to the Challenge website, forty thousand of whom cast votes for their favorite proposals.[49] GE has managed to build a fan base around the seemingly dull subject of the power grid.

The company has created so much value in the course of making profits and planning for the future that its contributions to society grow with their success and extend the company's influence well beyond its own operations and into the broader culture. That's what great brands do.

Making a Better World by Inspiring Widespread Change

Inspiring widespread change is the hallmark of a great brand. For Patagonia, making a positive impact on society is an ongoing, all-encompassing pursuit. Chouinard's commitment to social relevance for his company has extended far outside the walls of Patagonia. He once told the *Wall Street Journal*, "I never even wanted to be in business. . . . But I hang onto Patagonia because it's my resource to do something good. It's a way to demonstrate that corporations can lead examined lives."[50]

He has partnered with Walmart to help the company reduce packaging and water use in its supply chain. The two companies have joined to create a Sustainable Apparel Coalition, which now includes big brands such as Levi Strauss, Gap, and Nike. Together they've been developing new standards for producing clothing in an environmentally responsible way. "I adore Yvon," one Walmart executive told the *Wall Street Journal*. "When we went around together to get other companies on board, we code-named ourselves David and Goliath. Because in the realm of sustainability, we were David. Patagonia was Goliath."[51]

The builders of great brands including Chouinard drive the ecosystems around their companies to inspire substantive and sustaining change for all.

IKEA Improves People's Lives

From its humble inception in post–World War II Sweden, the IKEA brand has been about improving people's lives. The company is designed and operated with low prices at its core. IKEA's prices are low partly out of a competitive pricing strategy, but also out of the company commitment to a mission of widespread accessibility.[52]

"As a company, we have always been extremely clear about our ambition: to create a better life for people," says Ian Worling,

IKEA's director of business navigation. "That means we offer home furnishings at such low prices that as many people as possible can afford to buy them. That colors everything we do."[53]

While most retailers use design to justify higher prices, IKEA designers are directed to work in exactly the opposite way. Instead they use design to help secure the lowest possible price. IKEA designers conceive each IKEA product by starting with a functional need and a target price. Then they use their vast knowledge of innovative, low-cost manufacturing processes to create functional products, often coordinated in style. From there, large volumes are purchased to push prices down even further. Part of IKEA's design philosophy includes manufacturing products so they can be transported in flat packs and assembled at the customer's home. This design choice lowers prices even further by minimizing manufacturing, transportation, and storage costs. In this way, the IKEA concept uses design to ensure that IKEA products can be purchased and enjoyed by as many people as possible.[54]

IKEA also keeps prices low by enabling customers to make most purchase decisions themselves, thus optimizing the company's labor investment. They've made it easy to choose the right products by displaying them correctly, describing them accurately, packaging them for immediate self-service pickup, and offering a simple returns policy.[55]

At the same time, IKEA stresses the importance of product quality and minimal impact on the environment as also being critical to fulfilling the company's mission of life betterment. Suppliers must meet rigid standards that ensure sustainability and an overall beneficial effect.[56]

IKEA eliminates any unnecessary costs for production and warehousing through its flat packages. For example, by packing its HOTT kettle with some of the kettles upside down, the company is able to fit ten kettles in a box instead of six. By minimizing wasted space and increasing the filling rate in shipping containers in this way, IKEA simultaneously lowers prices for its customers and reduces the amount of packaging materials needed.[57]

Even IKEA's store design reflects a consciousness about its various stakeholders. Newer IKEA stores make more use of glass, both for aesthetic and functional reasons. Skylights are also now common in its self-serve warehouses. More natural light reduces energy costs, improves worker morale, and gives a better impression of the product.[58]

Inside and outside its four walls, IKEA's approaches create shared value for multiple stakeholder groups and enable the company to fulfill its mission of improving people's lives.

Changing the Way People Eat

Meanwhile, in Palo Alto, California, McDonald's restaurant veteran Mike Roberts is taking on one of the most ambitious start-ups to date: a fast food chain with a bold social vision of healthy food produced sustainably.

LYFE Kitchen, opened in 2011, was conceived as the Whole Foods of restaurants. It uses no butter, no cream, no white sugar, no white flour, no high-fructose corn syrup, no genetically modified food, no trans fats, no additives. All the cookies are dairy-free, all the beef from grass-fed, humanely raised cattle.[59] The building design and materials reflect a commitment to environmental and social sustainability concerns. Its packaging is from renewable sources and is compostable, and crew uniforms are made of 100 percent organic cotton or 91 percent recycled polyester.[60]

Roberts envisions Brussels sprouts as a healthy alternative to French fries. "I believe it to my core," he told *Wired* magazine. "People say, 'I have not had a Brussels sprout in 10 years, but I will have these four times a week.'" Roberts also believes that if Whole Foods could make a market of health-conscious consumers, seemingly out of nowhere, so can he and his team of ex-McDonald's restaurant pros. Even though it's early to be promoting the sure success of healthy fast food, Roberts admits, "There are 80 million people who have become much more aware of the food they eat. And that's going to continue as far out as we can see."[61]

For all the values relevance LYFE offers at its restaurants, the company's social aspirations are even higher. Roberts doesn't just want to build a sustainable, healthy brand of fast food—he wants LYFE to do for responsibly grown meat and vegetables what McDonald's did for factory-farmed beef. He has taken it as his mission to transform the way the world produces organic ingredients, so he's working with farmers, growers, and distributors to design an entirely new agricultural system and supply chain. And since Roberts was a McDonald's executive, he has a very good idea how to go about it.[62]

In this age of transforming the world through social efforts, LYFE might be an idea whose time has come.

Back to the Beginning

Perhaps no company has embraced creating shared value as thoroughly and for as long as Ben & Jerry's ice cream. It was a pioneer in the corporate social responsibility movement, and it continues to take socially and politically controversial stands today, despite being a wholly owned subsidiary of Unilever since 2000, because of the strong integration of the Ben & Jerry's brand with its social relevance. The company's social mission goals for 2011 included to "make ice cream that's aligned with our values" and "take the lead in promoting global sustainable dairy practices."[63]

"Making and selling the highest quality ice cream profitably in a competitive marketplace is not easy," CEO Jostein Solheim wrote in an annual report. "But doing it in line with our Social

Mission requires extraordinary commitment and passion from everyone in the Ben & Jerry's community."[64]

This brings us back to the first principle mentioned in this book: "Great Brands Start Inside"—they start brand building with company culture. Now at the end of the seventh principle, you can see that creating shared value is an inside job, too.

Great brands with Level 5 Relevance also have enormously strong internal cultures—cultures so strong that they extend through everything those great brands do, all the way through avoiding selling products, ignoring trends, refusing to chase customers, sweating the small stuff, and staying committed. All these principles end up achieving a social impact as the brands exert their power in society. If you're touching people emotionally, you're enriching their lives. If you avoid chasing customers, you'll have a more meaningful impact on the lives of those who share your values. If you sweat the small stuff, it's because you know that everything communicates, even the social programs that might not have immediate, measurable impacts on sales. And when you commit and stay committed, you build trust, the glue of any society.

Great brands never need to give back because they are so deeply involved in society already that they have no need to try to pick up anything and offer it; in the words of John Muir, they are already "hitched to everything else in the universe."[65]

The Eighth Principle
Brand as Business

What is the one quality that ultimately separates all great brands from the rest?

I call it the eighth principle: "Great Brands Do Brand as Business." The brand-as-business management approach has been woven throughout this book, and it knits together the seven principles; in fact, it systematically integrates them to produce business growth and brand strength.

Every great brand defines its brand *as* its business. It puts its brand at the core of the business and goes to great lengths to make sure there is no daylight between managing the brand and managing the business. In my experience, what separates a truly great brand from a merely good one is whether the organization carries out a complete and thorough implementation of the seven brand-building principles within a cohesive brand-as-business approach.

The trouble inherent in presenting these seven principles in discrete chapters is that it's very easy to see each of them as a stand-alone strategy, as if the book represented a menu of seven attractive optional measures. The eighth principle sets that straight. The eighth principle asserts that the first seven principles represent parts of an integrated, indivisible whole. Each principle relates to, supports, and explains the need for the others.

It's all too tempting as you read the preceding chapters to cherry-pick the two or three principles that resonate most or do most to flatter your personal strengths and abilities. You may experience the natural and understandable tendency to gloss over the ones that you think you're already doing well, and avoid altogether the ones that seem too difficult to implement, given your current circumstances. But the principles that seem the most obvious—and on the other hand, those that appear most challenging—are usually the very ones you really need to work on.

With the eighth principle, "Great Brands Do Brand as Business," it becomes clear how implementing the first seven principles is a progressive three-step approach to managing your business: culture, planning, and execution.

Culture. The process begins with the first principle, "Great Brands Start Inside," because a vital, vibrant culture unifies, aligns, focuses, motivates, and propels all your stakeholders forward. Culture provides the strong and necessary foundation needed to undertake every aspect of the brand-as-business approach—starting with high-level strategies and moving all the way through to detailed decision making.

Planning. Each of the next three principles informs some aspect of your critical business planning: making choices about which activities to do and not do. They help you apply your brand as that superior decision-making guiding light, consistent with the values and attributes set by your brand culture. Avoiding selling products informs the fundamental business question of what business you are in. The commitment to ignore trends turns your conversations about innovation and growth back to where they belong, guided by your culture and emotional connections to your customers. And by declining to chase after customers, you set the planning capstone by deciding who you want to attract, the customers for whom your brand exists.

Execution. Your culture and plans reach their ultimate fulfillment through the final three principles. Sweating the small stuff produces the fruits of operational excellence. Committing and staying committed ensures your execution remains focused and disciplined. And when you shift your emphasis to creating shared value for all your stakeholders, including your community and our planet, you execute with the greatest impact your brand can attain. Reaching for that goal (which, like any ideal, is never fully achievable) will strengthen your culture immeasurably, setting the stage for the next round of growth and success.

The seven principles form a holistic progression from setting what you believe to choosing what you will and will not do to engaging what you do at the highest level—demonstrating that it is a cohesive, integrated approach—doing brand as business, the eighth overarching principle—that maximizes the full power of them all.

Brand as business is what great brands do.

Brand Building Trumps Branding

Today's savvy consumers are likely to see through the brand façade behind which so many companies have hidden for years. They can easily find out if the business practices, products, and people behind a brand are what its ads say they are. And they're more likely to trust their own experience or the recommendation of a friend or even an online reviewer than a company's own chest thumping.

In fact, one could argue that the historical role brands have played—serving as symbols to guarantee a certain level of quality—is no longer relevant or useful today.

But that is not to say that brands themselves are no longer valuable. Though some have declared the death of branding, that might be true only if by *branding* they mean the practices of creating an image to serve as the face of a company, refreshing a logo or tagline in an attempt to reinvigorate the business, and developing advertising campaigns to "get our name out there." The business value of all these efforts is in decline and will continue to decline.

Operationalizing your brand creates and sustains real value. Your brand can't just be a promise; it must be a promise delivered.

In the Introduction, I discuss the critical importance of the way brand spending is budgeted and managed within an organization's structure. All too often, traditional branding activities such as advertising and public relations are seen as nice-to-have budget items that can be cut to save money when circumstances require it. Brand strategy is rarely aligned with other functional strategies. Brand-building investments are almost always narrowly focused on traditional marketing activities, with little impact on customer service, employee training, human resources, and the thousands of touchpoints that affect each customer's appraisal of the brand.

Great brands use the brand-as-business approach to avoid making these kinds of mistakes. With brand as business, the expenses of building the brand are usually indistinguishable from the expenses of building the business. Brand investments are integrated into business plans. Executives are evaluated on the return on those investments and business units are expected to participate in brand development.

Creating Real Business Value

Great brands use brand as business to re-ignite their organizations and create real business value in four ways.

- *To expose new growth opportunities.* Brand as business reframes what business the company is really in. By considering the bundle of values and attributes that comprise the value delivered to customers, the brand-as-business approach provides new innovation guardrails and a fresh perspective on potential areas for expansion, mergers, and acquisitions.

Consider how the multibillion-dollar online retailer Zappos started as an online shoe retailer, but because its leadership defined its brand more broadly ("a service company that happens to sell shoes"), its operating model has proven flexible enough to embrace a broad range of products. The company has successfully extended its offering into apparel, accessories, and even sporting goods and sporting gear.

- *To shape business objectives and strategies.* Brand as business uses brand positioning to evaluate current performance and prioritize possible new directions. Disparate groups can draw on their unified, well-defined culture and practices to develop a shared understanding of what needs to be done to achieve a stronger competitive position.

I once worked with a leading agricultural company that reconceived its brand in order to unite and align distributed sales and product teams. The new brand prescribed the way the products and services across the company's divisions and regions would be integrated into a unique and valuable solution for customers. This served as the basis for developing shared goals, an integrated sales process, and a robust innovation pipeline. The new brand strategy ultimately attracted a large conglomerate which acquired the company for a significant premium.

- *To create unified, focused, and integrated teams.* Brand as business encourages the use of the brand's values to inform and influence employee recruiting, training, development, and compensation and reward programs. Not only does this reduce operating costs through better employee selection and retention, it contributes to the development of high-performing teams. Better decisions are made more quickly and executed with excellence.

At Sony's electronics company, the brand management and organizational development groups worked closely to nurture a brand-building mindset throughout the organization. Through the deployment of a Brand Toolbox and Brand Engagement Sessions, people learned how their departments and workgroups supported the brand and how to work together to design more profitable strategic alliances, deliver more persuasive sales pitches, and devise new services and solutions to generate incremental revenue.

- *To connect the daily activities of every employee to the customer, to the bigger picture, and to longer-term business objectives.* Employees are more engaged, motivated, and productive in a brand-as-business workplace culture because they learn the meaning and purpose of their work. When the employee experience and the customer experience are inspired and guided by the same cultural values, employees discover and appreciate their roles in interpreting and reinforcing the brand in their actions and daily decision making.

Every year, Sharp Healthcare, San Diego's leading health care system, holds its All-Staff Assembly as a way to engage everyone who works on Sharp in recommitting to "the purpose and worth of our work and the difference we make in the lives of others." The result is a strong culture that inspires employees to deliver the Sharp Experience, the organization's brand vision and commitment to transforming the health care experience. It makes a difference in how Sharp people interact with and serve their patients, their affiliated physicians, and each other every day.

The Sharp Experience is credited with producing numerous advances in clinical outcomes, patient safety enhancements, and organizational and service improvements.[1]

Executing the Brand-as-Business Approach

Achieving these types of outcomes is usually the result of a disciplined process and development of core brand-building competencies. This is one of the pivotal areas where the promise of brand as business can drown in competing, everyday organizational contingencies. As a leader, you must be vigilant about removing potential barriers and zero in on the rigor of implementation.

Of the eleven core competencies identified in brand strategy implementation, research has found that these four are most highly correlated with successful implementation:[2]

- *Strategy implementation knowledge:* Your organization's ability to maintain, augment, and make available to its members the organization's knowledge on successful brand strategy implementation.
- *Implementation planning:* Your organization's ability to conceive implementation processes that achieve the brand strategy's goals effectively and efficiently.
- *Process coordination:* Your organization's ability to align implementation activities effectively, providing information to and exchanging information with stakeholders concerning how they can contribute to and support strategy implementation efforts.
- *Strategy translation:* Your organization's ability to convey a strategy's content to stakeholders who are relevant to successful implementation of the strategy.

Executing on these four competencies will put you way ahead of the game in both re-igniting your brand and aligning your organization with the brand-as-business approach. When a great brand nurtures implementation of its brand platform in these specific ways, it is really nurturing its culture, the foundation upon which everything else rests.

Using the Seven Principles to Trouble-Shoot Your Business

Brand as business is a universal approach. It is relevant to virtually all business problems and its methodologies and tools apply to a broad range of types of organizations. Brand as business can help you frame your response to some of the most common business issues, even those that don't allow the proper investment of time and resources to fully implement a brand-as-business approach. Here are a dozen prevalent business issues (some of which are probably awaiting you in the morning), and some suggestions on how the brand-as-business approach can help reframe them.

- *We're not growing as fast as we want to.* The brand-as-business management approach fosters customer intimacy, so you're able to create more pull in the market, instead of relying on push tactics. As discussed in Chapter Two, when you address the question "what business are we really in?" in a broader, more emotionally resonant way, you not only capture untapped share in your current category but also unlock potential growth in new ones. You strengthen your value proposition so that you generate incremental market demand.

- *We're losing share to competitors, including private labels.* Brand as business improves the development and delivery of your key differentiators so that you can ward off competitive encroachment. Principle Two, "Great Brands Avoid Selling Products," outlines how emotional connections elevate your brand above price wars and feature comparisons. Principle Three, "Great Brands

Ignore Trends," explains an even more distinctive approach, advancing cultural movements.

- *We need to do more with less.* Brand as business helps your organization become more efficient—you're able to focus your operating system on delivering value to your ideal customers, as discussed in Chapter Four, "Great Brands Don't Chase Customers," and to divest or deemphasize ancillary activities. You don't burn resources on distractions and opportunistic trends, as Principle Three instructs, and you avoid costly churn by committing to certain values and a specific direction over the long term, as discussed in Chapter Six, "Great Brands Commit and Stay Committed." By sweating the small stuff, Principle Five, you focus on the real driver of brand image—customer experience—and build your brand without large advertising and promotional budgets.

- *We need to deliver a more consistent customer experience.* As indicated in Chapter Five, brand as business encourages the alignment of all of your brand touchpoints and consistent brand delivery in every touchpoint. The execution tools in the brand-as-business approach facilitate one clear, consistent, common understanding of your brand among all stakeholders so they work together to deliver on it across customer experiences.

- *We aren't as innovative as the current environment requires.* Today, identifying new ways to grow requires a deeper, more intuitive customer understanding that enables you to anticipate needs and create markets. The anthropological research methodologies introduced in Chapter Two allow you to dig beneath the surface with customers and develop proprietary market insights to drive innovation.

- *We can't decide which customer segments to prioritize.* The Customer Experience Architecture tool described in Chapter Five helps you identify and prioritize which customers and customer experiences are most valuable by applying brand-based criteria. It also unifies and integrates all the customer experiences you offer into a cohesive framework that creates synergies between efforts directed toward disparate segments.

• *Social media activity is causing us to lose control over how our brand is perceived.* By putting your brand at the center of your business and using it to drive everything you do, you eliminate any disconnect between what you say and what you do. This is why great brands start inside (Chapter One). Moreover, brand as business helps you control the things you can, by applying tools and processes that facilitate on-brand execution—and it positions your organization well for the things you can't control by ensuring brand integrity when your company is put under the microscope of inquiring consumers.

• *Employee morale is low.* Brand as business gives employees' work a more meaningful purpose and helps people understand the importance of their role in building the brand. By following Principle One, starting inside and engaging employees with the brand, you connect what they do on a daily basis to the bigger picture and longer-term objectives. This sustains morale far longer than perks and parties.

• *We don't have a systematic process for evaluating new business opportunities.* The brand-as-business management approach introduces a brand ethic to corporate planning and new business decision making. The approach in Chapter Four guides the development of your competitive brand positioning and Chapter Six outlines several methods for clarifying your brand essence. Together, these elements comprise your brand platform, which integrates brand understanding and business strategy and serves as a tool for evaluating new opportunities. The result is a clear and efficient approach that can be applied consistently.

• *Not everyone shares the same vision for the business.* The brand-as-business management approach includes developing a Brand Toolbox, which enables you to inform, inspire, and instruct all your stakeholders on what the brand stands for, how to interpret and reinforce it in their daily decision making, and how it might evolve over time. Brand Engagement Sessions get people excited about working on the brand and help them identify decisions and behaviors that are aligned with the brand's message. Both of these are described in Chapter One.

- *Out in the marketplace, there are misperceptions about who we are and what we do.* By starting inside, brand as business fosters internal brand clarity and alignment, which serve as the foundation for the external brand understanding you desire. You are then able to articulate to the outside world the role and value of your brand in a clear and compelling way—and ensure your brand is communicated and delivered consistently at every touchpoint (salespeople, advertising, service representatives, media relations, and the rest).

- *Our ability to predict the future has diminished.* In today's ever-changing business climate, being ready for the future relies less on strategic planning and more on laying the foundation for strategic thinking and actions when changes occur. Brand as business replaces a rigid, point-in-time planning process with an emphasis on shared cultural values and brand understanding that can be applied and reapplied as needed. Using your brand as the key decision filter about product, service, and customer development provides a superior means to make planning decisions because it is more flexible, outcome-oriented, and driven by a unifying, big picture.

The Challenge of Brand Leadership

Brand as business is not business as usual. Most companies don't operate this way.

To apply the eighth principle, you as a leader must explicitly decide, articulate, and adopt your brand as the driver of every aspect of your business. Brand building must shift from a strategic function to an orchestration function—from simply setting direction to facilitating implementation across all functions, all stakeholders. You must use it to nurture a culture that differentiates the company, conveys value beyond any single product or service, and forms a valuable bond with customers. Brand as business needs to be owned by you and others at the highest levels of the organization. It can't be delegated to your marketing department or your advertising agency. It must be driven—and embraced—as an enterprise-wide approach.

Try to remember that your brand is a verb. Your brand is not your image, your brand is what you do. Brands are about action, not advertising. Your brand is in constant motion, constantly evolving. Try to think of it not as an identity to lean on but as an instrument to be put to use.

The fundamental difference between building great brands and old-style branding becomes clearer every day—with the dramatic changes in the economy and ground-breaking developments in technology and communications, old-style branding may be dead. But brands are now more important than ever.

Your organization must step back from using your brand as a static outward-facing, image-oriented object. No longer is your brand an experience mediated through messaging and marketing communications. Your brand is the experience that is actually delivered and communicated through every single thing you do, every day, around the clock.

That's what great brands do.

Notes

Introduction

1. Huxley, Aldous. "Case of Voluntary Ignorance," *Collected Essays* (New York: HarperCollins, 1959). Aldous Huxley: *"That men do not learn very much from the lessons of history is the most important of all the lessons of history."*

2. Ries, Al. "Marketing Myth-Busting: Kodak Wasn't Slow to Digital; It Was the First One In," *Advertising Age*, January 19, 2012. http://adage.com /article/al-ries/marketing-myth-busting-kodak-digital/232226/.

3. Kucera, Danielle, and Rita Nazareth. "Kodak Worth More in Breakup with $3 Billion Patents," *Bloomberg*, August 17, 2011. http://www.bloom berg.com/news/2011-08-17/kodak-worth-five-times-more-in-breakup -with-3-billion-patents-real-m-a.html. "The Last Kodak Moment," *Economist*, January 14, 2012. http://www.economist.com/node/21542796.

4. Vivaldi Partners. "Social Currency," 2010. http://images.fastcompany .com/Vivald-iPartners_Social-Currency.pdf.

5. Gerzema, John. "Energized Differentiation," proprietary report, Brand Asset Consulting, November 2011.

6. Interbrand website. "The Best Global Brands 2012," available at: http:// www.interbrand.com/en/best-global-brands/2012/Best-Global -Brands-2012.aspx. Millward Brown website. "The Stengel 50," avail- able at: http://www.millwardbrown.com/Sites/Brand_Ideal/The_Study. aspx. *Fortune* website. "Best Companies to Work For," available at: http:// money.cnn.com/magazines/fortune/best-companies/.

7. Phang, Llew-Ann. "ANA/Interbrand: Seniors Marketers Blind to Brand Value," *Marketing-Interactive*, October 24, 2008. http://www.marketing-interactive.com/news/9286.

8. Macarthur, Kate. "Vowing Turnaround, Gap Dubs 2007 a 'Transitional Year,'" *Advertising Age*, March 6, 2007. http://adage.com/article/news/vowing-turnaround-gap-dubs-2007-a-transitional-year/115411/.

9. (RED) news release. "(RED) Room Showcasing Annie Leibovitz Photography Opens for World Aids Day at the National Portrait Gallery," November 26, 2008. http://www.joinred.com/press_releases/red-room-showcasing-annie-leibovitz-photography-opens-for-world-aids-day-at-the-national-portrait-gallery/. Frazier, Mya. "Costly Red Campaign Reaps Meager $18 Million," *Advertising Age*, March 5, 2007. http://adage.com/article/news/costly-red-campaign-reaps-meager-18-million/115287/.

10. Gap Inc. 2007 Annual Report. http://media.corporate-ir.net/media_files/IROL/11/111302/AR07.pdf.

11. Kerner, Noah, Gene Pressman, and Andrew Essex. *Chasing Cool: Standing Out in Today's Cluttered Marketplace* (New York: Atria, 2007).

12. Vranica, Suzanne, and Robert A. Guth. "Microsoft Enlists Jerry Seinfeld in Its Ad Battle Against Apple," *Wall Street Journal*, August 21, 2008. http://online.wsj.com/article/SB121928939429159525.html.

13. Stone, Brad. "In Campaign Wars, Apple Still Has Microsoft's Number," *New York Times*, February 3, 2009. http://www.nytimes.com/2009/02/04/business/media/04adco.html?_r=0.

14. Larreche, J. C. (2008). *The Momentum Effect: How to Ignite Exceptional Growth* (Upper Saddle River, NJ: Wharton School).

15. Ferdows, Kasra, Michael A. Lewis, and Jose A. D. Machuca. "Rapid-Fire Fulfillment," *Harvard Business Review*, November 2004.

16. Neate, Rupert. "Kodak Falls in the 'Creative Destruction of the Digital Age,'" *Guardian*, January 19, 2012. http://www.guardian.co.uk/business/2012/jan/19/kodak-bankruptcy-protection.

17. Mui, Chunka. "How Kodak Failed," *Forbes*, January 18, 2012. http://www.forbes.com/sites/chunkamui/2012/01/18/how-kodak-failed/.

18. Scheyder, Ernest. "Focus on Glory Kept Kodak from Digital Win," *Reuters*, January 19, 2012. http://www.reuters.com/article/2012/01/19/us-kodak-bankruptcy-idUSTRE80I1N020120119.

Chapter 1

1. "Samuel J. Palmisano," IBM website, October, 2012. http://www-03.ibm.com/press/us/en/biography/36420.wss.

2. Hemp, Paul, and Thomas A. Stewart. "Leading Change When Business Is Good," *Harvard Business Review*, December 2004.

3. "IBM Global Services: A Brief History," IBM website, n.d. http://www -03.ibm.com/ibm/history/documents/pdf/gservices.pdf.

4. Hemp and Stewart, "Leading Change When Business Is Good."

5. "IBM Basics," IBM website, n.d. http://www.ibm.com/ibm/responsibility /basics.shtml.

6. Silverthorne, Sean. "The Vanguard Corporation," Harvard Business School Working Knowledge (blog), October 5, 2009. http://hbswk.hbs .edu/item/6295.html.

7. Palmisano, Sam. "Our Values at Work on Being an IBMer," IBM website, n.d. http://www.ibm.com/ibm/values/us/.

8. Birkinshaw, Julian M. *Reinventing Management: Smarter Choices for Getting Work Done* (San Francisco: Jossey-Bass, 2010), pp. 100–102.

9. Ibid.

10. Palmisano, "Our Values at Work on Being an IBMer."

11. Ibid.

12. Fleming, John H., and Dan Witters. "Do Consumers 'Get' Your Brand?" *Gallup Business Journal*, February 29, 2012. http://businessjournal.gallup .com/content/153005/consumers-brand.aspx#1.

13. Ryan, Eric, Adam Lowry, and Lucas Conley. *The Method Method: 7 Obsessions That Helped Our Scrappy Start-up Turn an Industry Upside Down* (New York: Portfolio/Penguin, 2011).

14. Ibid.

15. Warner, Melanie. "Taming a Type-A Culture Gone Wild," *MoneyWatch*, November 24, 2009. http://www.cbsnews.com/8301-505125_162 -51367992/taming-a-type-a-culture-gone-wild/.

16. Ryan, Lowry, and Conley, *The Method Method*.

17. Taylor, Heather. "How to Evolve Your Brand and Logo the Starbucks Way," Econsultancy.com, September 13, 2012. http://econsultancy.com /us/blog/10702-how-to-evolve-your-brand-and-logo-the-starbucks-way.

18. Fleming and Witters, "Do Consumers 'Get' Your Brand?"

19. "IWAY, Our Code of Conduct," IKEA website, n.d. http://www.ikea.com /ms/en_US/about_ikea/our_responsibility/iway/index.html.

20. Hemp and Stewart, "Leading Change When Business Is Good."

21. Rohde, David. "The Anti-Walmart: The Secret Sauce of Wegmans Is People," *Atlantic*, March 23, 2012. http://www.theatlantic.com/business /archive/2012/03/the-anti-walmart-the-secret-sauce-of-wegmans-is -people/254994/#.

22. Prospero, Michael A. "Employee Innovator: Wegmans," *Fast Company*, October 1, 2004. http://www.fastcompany.com/51347 /employee-innovator-wegmans.
23. Rohde, "The Anti-Walmart."
24. Hemp, Stewart, "Leading Change When Business Is Good."
25. Useem, Jerry. "Jim Collins on Tough Calls," *Fortune*, June 27, 2005. http://money.cnn.com/magazines/fortune/fortune _archive/2005/06/27/8263408/index.htm.

Chapter 2

1. Bedbury, Scott, and Stephen Fenichell. *A New Brand World: 8 Principles for Achieving Brand Leadership in the 21st Century* (New York: Viking, 2002), pp. 32–37.
2. Ibid.
3. Gobé, Mark. "Brandjam: Humanizing Brands Through Emotional Design," NRF website, January 13, 2008. http://www.nrf.com /Attachments.asp?id=20455.
4. Kinnear, Simon. "Nike Beats Adidas to Olympic Buzz Monitoring Gold," McConnells Marketing News, February 16, 2012. http:// www.mccgp.co.uk/marketing-news/social-media-marketing /nike-beats-adidas-to-olympic-buzz-monitoring-gold/1133/.
5. Muschamp, Herbert. "Design Review; Seductive Objects with a Sly Sting," *New York Times*, July 2, 1999.
6. Brandau, Mark. "Factors Beyond Food Attract Millennial Diners," *Nation's Restaurant News*, May 11, 2012. http://nrn.com/latest-headlines /factors-beyond-food-attract-millennial-diners.
7. Stengel, Jim. "Chapter 7: How Pampers Changed the World," in *Grow: How Ideals Power Growth and Profit at the World's Greatest Companies* (New York: Crown Business, 2011).
8. Ibid.
9. Ryan, Thomas J. "Brand Strategy at Amazon.com," *Apparel*, March 3, 2006. http://apparel.edgl.com/news/Brand-Strategy-at-Amazon-com62944.
10. Dignan, Larry. "Amazon's Kindle Fire Economics: A Focus on Lifetime Value of Customer," *ZDNet.com*, October 26, 2011. http://www.zdnet .com/blog/btl/amazons-kindle-fire-economics-a-focus-on-lifetime-value -of-customer/61880.
11. Sawhney, Ravi. "How Do You Turn Your Customers into Brand Evangelists?" Co.DESIGN, June 23, 2011. http://www

.fastcodesign.com/1664135/how-do-you-turn-your-customers-into
-brand-evangelists.

12. "Research: Brand-Conscious Consumers Take Bad News to Heart," *News Bureau*, August 15, 2011. http://news.illinois.edu/news/11/0815brands
_TiffanyWhite.html.

13. Ibid.

14. Nudd, Tim. "How Nike+ Made 'Just Do It' Obsolete," *Adweek*, June 20, 2012. http://www.adweek.com/news/advertising-branding/how-nike
-made-just-do-it-obsolete-141252.

15. "List of All James Bond Movies," 007James website, n.d. http://
www.007james.com/articles/list_of_james_bond_movies.php?gclid=
CL3N9J_zrbkCFY5r7AodLSgAhw.

16. Nudd, "How Nike+ Made 'Just Do It' Obsolete."

17. "About Google," Google website, n.d. http://www.google.com/about
/company/.

18. Levitt, Theodore. "Marketing Myopia," *Harvard Business Review*, July 2004. Reprint available online: http://hbr.org/2004/07
/marketing-myopia/ar/1.

19. "Telstra to Apple: 'Stick to Your Knitting,'" *Age*, February 16, 2007. http://www.theage.com.au/news/biztech/telstra-to-apple-stick-to-your
-knitting/2007/02/15/1171405363291.html.

20. Bedbury and Fenichell, *A New Brand World*.

Chapter 3

1. Carr, David. "The Triumph of Avoiding the Traps," *New York Times*, November 23, 2009.

2. "Reebok Athletic Shoe Company a Step Ahead in America," *News & Courier/Evening Post*, August 18, 1985. http://news.google.com/newspape
rs?nid=2506&dat=19850818&id=NJJJAAAAIBAJ&sjid=PgwNAAAAIBAJ
&pg=992,5619203.

3. Brand, Rachel. "Chipotle Founder Had Big Dreams," *Rocky Mountain News*, December 23, 2006. http://www.rockymountainnews.com
/news/2006/dec/23/chipotle-founder-had-big-dreams/.

4. Ibid.

5. Kaplan, David A. "Chipotle's Growth Machine," *Fortune*, September 12, 2011. http://features.blogs.fortune.cnn.com/2011/09/12
/chipotles-growth-machine/.

6. Shambora, Jessica. "Chipotle: Rise of a Fast-Food Empire." *Fortune*, October 7, 2010. http://money.cnn.com/2010/10/06/smallbusiness /chipotle_started.fortune/index.htm.

7. Butler, Cherryh A. "Who Will Be 'the Chipotle' of the Pizza Industry?" Pizzamarketplace.com, July 28, 2011. http://www.pizzamarketplace.com /article/182852/Who-will-be-the-Chipotle-of-the-pizza-industry.

8. Gold, Jonathan. "The Fast-Food Revolutionary," *Wall Street Journal*, October 27, 2011. http://online.wsj.com/article/SB1000142405297020464 45045766535503294898570.html#ixzz2F7df7Kow. Jacobs, A. J. "Esquire's Most Inspiring CEO in America: Steve Ells, Founder and Co-CEO, Chipotle," *Esquire*, October 2012. http://www.esquire.com/features /most-inspiring-ceo-1012-steve-ells#slide-12.

9. Stein, Joel. "The Fast-Food Ethicist," *Time*, July 23, 2012. http://www .time.com/time/printout/0,8816,2119329,00.html.

10. Ibid.

11. Ibid.

12. Ibid.

13. Gold, "The Fast-Food Revolutionary."

14. Burnsed, Brian. "In the Luxury Sector, Discounting Can Be Dangerous," *BusinessWeek*, July 23, 2009. http://www.businessweek.com/magazine /content/09_31/b4141049551979.htm.

15. Guenette, Ryan. "Does Tiffany Have Any Sparkle Left?" *Motley Fool*, September 6, 2012. http://beta.fool.com/makinmoney2424/2012/09/06 /does-tiffany-have-any-sparkle-left/10704/.

16. Rosenbloom, Stephanie. "A Conference Makes Learning Free (and Sexy)," *New York Times*, September 24, 2010. http://www.nytimes .com/2010/09/26/fashion/26TEDX.html?_r=1&.

17. Kamenetz, Anya. "How TED Connects the Idea-Hungry Elite," *Fast Company*, September 1, 2010. http://www.fastcompany.com/1677383 /how-ted-connects-idea-hungry-elite.

18. Rosenbloom, "A Conference Makes Learning Free (and Sexy)."

19. Carr, "The Triumph of Avoiding the Traps."

20. Costa, Dan. "How Starbucks Created a Digital 'Third Place,'" *PC Magazine*, October 21, 2010. http://www.pcmag.com/arti cle2/0,2817,2371235,00.asp.

21. Hogan, Marc. "Gaga's New Album 'ARTPOP' Will Also Be App-Pop," *Spin*, September 6, 2012. http://www.spin.com/articles/lady-gagas -artpop-app.

22. Owens, Simon. "The Secrets of Lady Gaga's Social Media Success," *TNW: The Next Web*, March 15, 2011. http://thenextweb.com /media/2011/03/15/the-secrets-of-lady-gagas-social-media-success/. Lady Gaga Twitter account. http://twitter.com/LadyGaga.

23. Kim, W. Chan., and Renée Mauborgne. *Blue Ocean Strategy: How to Create Uncontested Market Space and Make the Competition Irrelevant* (Boston, MA: Harvard Business School, 2005).

24. Mackinnon, Lauchlan A. K. "Strategy's Strategist: An Interview with Richard Rumelt," *McKinsey Quarterly*, November 2007.

25. Zmuda, Natalie. "How Purpose Affects the Bottom Line," *Advertising Age*, October 8, 2012. http://adage.com/article/cmo-interviews /purpose-affects-bottom-line/237597/.

26. Buchanan, Leigh. "Zumba Fitness: Company of the Year," *Inc.*, December 4, 2012. http://www.inc.com/magazine/201212/leigh-buchanan/zumba -fitness-company-of-the-year-2012.html.

27. Gerzema, John, and Ed Lebar. "The Trouble with Brands," *Strategy+Business*, May 26, 2009. http://www.strategy-business.com /article/09205?pg=all.

Chapter 4

1. Mattioli, Dana. "Lululemon's Secret Sauce," *Wall Street Journal*, March 22, 2012. http://online.wsj.com/article/SB100014240527023038129045772 95882632723066.html.

2. Laura Klauberg, Senior Vice President, Brand and Community, Lululemon Athletica, personal interview with Denise Lee Yohn on January 4, 2013.

3. Sean O'Connor, Owner, Creative Leverage, personal interview with Denise Lee Yohn on December 6, 2012.

4. Malcolm, Hadley. "Lululemon Lovers Buy into Healthy Lifestyle," *USA Today*, March 19, 2013. http://www.usatoday.com/story/money /business/2013/03/19/lululemon-yoga-exercise-retail-running/1917659/.

5. Laura Klauberg, personal interview.

6. Ibid.

7. Widlitz, Stacey. "Lululemon Ducks the Radar and Lands in London," *Consumer Nation*, April 17, 2012. http://www.cnbc.com /id/47073651.

8. Morgan, Adam. *Eating the Big Fish: How Challenger Brands Can Compete Against Brand Leaders* (New York: Wiley, 1999).

9. Ibid.

10. "The Rolling Stones Biography," Rock and Roll Hall of Fame.com, n.d. http://rockhall.com/inductees/the-rolling-stones/bio/.

11. Baskin, Jonathan Salem. "The Branding Secrets of the Rolling Stones," Forbes.com, December 14, 2012. http://www.forbes.com/sites /jonathansalembaskin/2012/12/14/the-secrets-of-successful-branding -according-to-the-rolling-stones/.

12. Leopold, Todd. "Not 'the Last Rock 'n' Roll Band,'" CNN.com, January 4, 2006. http://www.cnn.com/2006/SHOWBIZ/Music/01/03/marah /index.html.

13. Gerzema, John, and Ed Lebar. "The Trouble with Brands," Strategy+Business, May 26, 2009. http://www.strategy-business.com /article/09205?pg=all.

14. Kowitt, Beth. "Inside the Secret World of Trader Joe's," Fortune, August 23, 2010. http://money.cnn.com/2010/08/20/news/companies/inside _trader_joes_full_version.fortune/index.htm#joe.

15. Ibid.

16. Ibid.

17. Mallinger, Mark, and Gerry Rossy. "The Trader Joe's Experience," Graziadio Business Review 10, no 2 (2007). http://gbr.pepperdine .edu/2010/08/the-trader-joes-experience/.

18. Ibid.

19. Garfield, Bob, and Doug Levy. Can't Buy Me Like: How Authentic Customer Connections Drive Superior Results (London: Portfolio Penguin, 2013).

20. Patton, Leslie, and Bryan Gruley. "Walter Robb on Whole Foods' Recession Lessons," Bloomberg Businessweek, August 9, 2012. http://www .businessweek.com/articles/2012-08-09/walter-robb-on-whole-foods -recession-lessons.

21. Ibid.

22. Flynn, Andrew, Jesse Purewal, and Mike Leiser. Prophet's 2011 State of Marketing Study, Prophet.com, June 7, 2011. http://www.prophet.com /thinking/view/586-prophets-2011-state-of-marketing-study.

23. Peter Fader, Frances and Pei-Yuan Chia Professor of Marketing, Wharton School of the University of Pennsylvania, personal interview with Denise Lee Yohn on March 9, 2012.

24. McDonald, Duff. "Red Bull's Billionaire Maniac," Bloomberg Businessweek, May 19, 2011. http://www.businessweek.com/magazine/content/11_22 /b4230064852768.htm.

25. Ibid.

26. Hollis, Nigel. "The Red Bull Case Study: Branding Not Marketing," MillwardBrown.com, June 13, 2007. http://www.millwardbrown.com /global/blog/Post/2007-06-13/The-Red-Bull-case-study-branding-not -marketing.aspx.

27. Ibid.

28. "Mission Complete: Red Bull Stratos Lands Safely Back on Earth," YouTube Official Blog, October 14, 2012. http://youtube-global.blogspot .ca/2012/10/mission-complete-red-bull-stratos-lands.html.

29. Red Bull website, www.redbullusa.com.

30. Hollis, "The Red Bull Case Study."

31. Hanna, Cheryl. "Building Customer Relationships Part of American Express Improved Services," Service Untitled, July 7, 2010. http://www .serviceuntitled.com/building-customer-relationships-part-of-american -express-improved-services/2010/07/07/.

32. Levere, Jane L. "The Right Plastic for Perks," *New York Times*, May 16, 2011. http://www.nytimes.com/2011/05/17/business/17travel .html?pagewanted=all.

33. Suther, Tim. "Not All Consumers Are Created Equal," *Advertising Age*, June 26, 2012. http://adage.com/article/cmo-strategy /customers-created-equal/235361/.

34. Rifkin, Glenn. "How Richard Branson Works Magic," *Strategy+Business*, October 1, 1998. http://www.strategy-business.com /article/13416?gko=19354.

35. Branson, Richard. "Richard Branson on Winning Customers' Trust," *Entrepreneur*, March 1, 2011. http://www.entrepreneur.com /article/219230.

36. Branson, Richard. "Richard Branson on the Secret to Exceeding Customer Expectations," *Entrepreneur*, July 16, 2012. http://www .entrepreneur.com/article/223969.

37. *Entrepreneur*, March 30, 2011. Edited excerpt from Richard Branson, *Business Stripped Bare: Adventures of a Global Entrepreneur* (London: Virgin Books, 2010).

Chapter 5

1. Nelson, Emily, and Sarah Ellison. "In a Shift, Marketers Beef Up Ad Spending Inside Stores," *Wall Street Journal*, September 21, 2005. http:// online.wsj.com/article/0,,SB112725891535046751,00.html.

2. Ibid.

3. Brown, Bruce, and Scott D. Anthony. "How P&G Tripled Its Innovation Success Rate," *Harvard Business Review*, June 2011.

4. Byran, Lori. "Knowing the Consumer Is Part of the Package," *CPC Packaging*, November/December 2002. http://www.cpcpkg.com /magazine/02_11_packager.php.

5. Isaacson, Walter. *Steve Jobs* (New York: Simon & Schuster, 2012), p. 78.

6. Ibid., p. 347.

7. Gruley, Brian. "At Chobani, the Turkish King of Greek Yogurt," *Bloomberg Businessweek*, January 31, 2013. http://www.businessweek.com /articles/2013-01-31/at-chobani-the-turkish-king-of-greek-yogurt.

8. Rogowski, Ron. "Forrester's Ron Rogowski: Introducing Emotional Experience Design," 1to1 Media Blog, October 28, 2009. http:// www.1to1media.com/weblog/2009/10/forresters_ron_rogowski_introd .html.

9. Uncommon Goods website. http://uncommongoods.com.

10. Clarke, Emma. "Wake Up and Smell the Freesia," CNN.com, October 5, 2007. http://www.cnn.com/2007/BUSINESS/10/05/smell.marketing/.

11. "Starwood Details Clear Strategies for Its 8 Brands; New Signature Service Elements Created in Each Brand," Hotel Online, May 23, 2006. http://www.hotel-online.com/News/PR2006_2nd/May06 _StarwoodStrategy.html.

12. Sabrina Wiewel, Chief Tax Network Officer, H&R Block, speaking at Forrester Research's Customer Experience Forum 2010, June 30, 2010.

13. Overholt, Alison. "Smart Strategies: Putting Ideas to Work," *Fast Company*, April 1, 2004. http://www.fastcompany.com/49233 /smart-strategies-putting-ideas-work.

14. Jones, Jeanne Lang. "Questions for: Sally Jewell," *Puget Sound Business Journal*, December 9, 2011. http://www.bizjournals.com/seattle/print -edition/2011/12/09/questions-for-sally-jewell-chief.html?page=all.

15. Flynn, Andrew, Jesse Purewal, and Mike Leiser. "Prophet's 2011 State of Marketing Study," Prophet, June 7, 2011. http://www.prophet.com /thinking/view/586-prophets-2011-state-of-marketing-study.

16. Baker, Rosie. "Marketers Must Fix Disconnect Between Brand Promise and Experience," *MarketingWeek*, July 17, 2012. http://www .marketingweek.co.uk/news/brands-must-match-experience-to -marketing/4002764.article.

17. Wilson, Marianne. "IBM Study: All Consumers Looking for a Consistent Experience, from Start to Finish," *Chain Store Age*, December 11, 2012. http://chainstoreage.com/article/ibm-study-all-consumers-looking -consistent-experience-start-finish.

18. Mellor, Nathan. "Customer-Service at Chick-fil-A," Character First Online Library, n.d. http://library.characterfirst.com/qualities/availability /customer-service/.

19. Salter, Chuck. "Chick-fil-A's Recipe for Customer Service," *Fast Company*, 2004. http://www.fastcompany.com/resources/customer/chickfila.html.

20. "Highlights and Awards," Chick-fil-A website, 2013. http://www.chick-fil -a.com/Company/Highlights-Awards#?award-slider=2.

21. "Retaining Your Best Hourly Workers," Workforce Institute, February, 2008. http://www.workforceinstitute.org/wp-content/uploads/2008/02 /Intro-to-book07.pdf.

22. Salter, "Chick-fil-A's Recipe for Customer Service."

23. Bliss, Jeanne. "Customers Defect When the Silos Don't Connect," CustomerBliss.com, n.d. http://www.customerbliss.com/news/7/97 /Customers-Defect-When-the-Silos-Don-t-Connect.htm.

24. Starmer, Samantha. "The Holistic Customer: Beyond the Website Experience—Managing Experience 2010," Slideshare.net, April 27, 2010. http://www.slideshare.net/samanthastarmer/the-holistic-customer -beyond-the-website-experience.

25. Porterfield, Elaine. "How REI became the Most-Respected Private Company Brand in Washington." *Puget Sound Business Journal*, July 29, 2011. http://www.bizjournals.com/seattle/print-edition/2011/07/29 /how-rei-became-the-most-respected.html?page=all.

26. Potter, Everett. "World's Best Airlines," *Travel+Leisure*, November 27, 2012. http://travel.yahoo.com/ideas/world-s-best-airlines.html.

27. Heracleous, L., and J. Wirtz. "Strategy and Organization at Singapore Airlines: Achieving Sustainable Advantage Through Dual Strategy." *Journal of Air Transport Management*, 2009, doi:10.1016/j .jairtraman.2008.11.011.

28. Ibid.

29. Roll, Martin. "Singapore Airlines—an Excellent Asian Brand," Venture Republic, n.d. http://www.venturerepublic.com/resources/singapore _airlines_-_an_excellent_asian_brand.asp.

30. Heracleous and Wirtz, "Strategy and Organization at Singapore Airlines."

31. Ibid.

32. Roll, "Singapore Airlines—an Excellent Asian Brand."

33. Taylor, Bill. "Why Zappos Pays New Employees to Quit—and You Should Too," *Harvard Business Review*, May 2012.

34. Charleton, Graham. "Q&A: Zappos' Jane Judd on Customer Loyalty," *Econsultancy*, November 4, 2009. http://econsultancy.com/us /blog/4912-q-a-zappos-jane-judd-on-customer-loyalty.

35. "Live from ANA: Zappos.com Cultivates Customer Service," *Chief Marketer*, April 18, 2008. http://chiefmarketer.com/news/live-ana-zap -poscom-cultivates-customer-service. "Zappos Core Values," Zappos website. http://about.zappos.com/our-unique-culture/zappos-core-values.

Chapter 6

1. Haden, Jeff. "Shake Shack CEO: 'We Want to Be the Anti-Chain Chain.'" *Inc.*, July 16, 2012. http://www.inc.com/jeff-haden/shake-shack-ceo-the -anti-chain-burger-chain.html.

2. Randall Garutti, CEO, Shake Shack, personal interview with Denise Lee Yohn on November 20, 2012.

3. Collins, James C., and Jerry I. Porras. *Built to Last: Successful Habits of Visionary Companies* (New York: HarperBusiness, 1994) p. 54.

4. Collins, Jim, and Jerry Porras. "Building Your Company's Vision," *Harvard Business Review*, September 1996. http://hbr.org/1996/09 /building-your-companys-vision/ar/1.

5. Keller, Kevin. "The New Branding Imperatives: Insights for the New Marketing Realities," Marketing Science Institute, 2010. http://www.msi .org/publications/publication.cfm?pub=1744.

6. Markides, Constantinos. "A Dynamic View of Strategy," *MIT Sloan Management Review*, April 15, 1999. http://sloanreview.mit.edu /article/a-dynamic-view-of-strategy.

7. Blumber, Alex, and David Kestenbaum. "Economy Got You Down? Many Blame Rating Firms," *Morning Edition*, National Public Radio, June 5, 2009.

8. Davenport, Tom. "The Anti-Goldman Culture," *Harvard Business Review* Blog Network, March 15, 2012. http://blogs.hbr.org/cs/2012/03/the_anti -goldman_culture.htm.

9. Zook, Chris. "Good Strategy's Non-Negotiables," *Harvard Business Review* Blog Network, March 15, 2012. http://blogs.hbr.org/ideacast/2012/03 /good-strategys-non-negotiables.html.

10. "Repeatability Cycle," Bain & Company, n.d. http://repeatability.com /design-principles/repeatability-cycle.aspx.

11. Davenport, "The Anti-Goldman Culture."

12. Quittner, Josh. "The Charmed Life of Amazon's Jeff Bezos," CNNMoney. April 15, 2008. http://money.cnn.com/2008/04/14/news/companies /quittner_bezos.fortune/.

13. O'Sullivan, Kate. "Kremed!" *CFO Magazine*, June 1, 2005. http://www .cfo.com/article.cfm/4007436.

14. Farzad, Roben. "Krispy Kreme's Unlikely Comeback," *Bloomberg Businessweek*. February 22, 2013. http://www.businessweek.com /articles/2013-02-22/krispy-kremes-unlikely-comeback.

15. O'Sullivan, "Kremed!"

16. Collins and Porras, "Building Your Company's Vision."

17. Bezos, Jeff. 2012 Letter to Shareholders, Amazon.com, April 2013. http:// www.sec.gov/Archives/edgar/data/1018724/000119312513151836 /d511111dex991.htm.

18. "Jeff Bezos on Leading for the Long-Term at Amazon," *Harvard Business Review* Blog Network, January 3, 2013. http://blogs.hbr.org/ideacast /2013/01/jeff-bezos-on-leading-for-the.html.

19. Randall Garutti, personal interview.

20. Ibid.

21. Thomas Edison maintained that genius was "1 percent inspiration and 99 percent perspiration," and that applies to most desirable and creative qualities, including invention and brand clarity.

22. Mouawad, Jad. "Pushing 40, Southwest Is Still Playing the Rebel," *New York Times*, November 20, 2010. http://www.nytimes.com/2010/11/21 /business/21south.html?pagewanted=all.

23. Morgan, Adam. *Eating the Big Fish: How Challenger Brands Can Compete Against Brand Leaders* (New York: Wiley, 1999).

24. Ibid.

25. Ibid.

26. Ibid.

27. "Our Credo," Johnson & Johnson website, n.d. http://www.jnj.com /connect/about-jnj/jnj-credo/.

28. Rehak, Judith. "Tylenol Made a Hero of Johnson & Johnson," *New York Times*, March 23, 2002. http://www.nytimes.com/2002/03/23/your -money/23iht-mjj_ed3_.html.

29. Ibid.

30. Collins, Jim. *Good to Great: Why Some Companies Make the Leap . . . and Others Don't* (New York: HarperCollins, 2001).

31. "Our Foundation Principles," Container Store website. http://standfor .containerstore.com/our-foundation-principles/.

32. Breen, Bill. "The Lamest Question in Retail Is, 'Can I Help You?'" *Fast Company*, December 31, 2002. http://www.fastcompany.com/45843 /whats-selling-america-part-5–5.

33. Ibid.

34. Bryant, Adam. "Three Good Hires? He'll Pay More for One Who's Great," *New York Times*, March 13, 2010. http://www.nytimes .com/2010/03/14/business/14corners.html?pagewanted=all.

35. Ibid.

36. 2012 sales: "Container Store Leaps to Top Spot by Being Employee-Centric," *Dallas Morning News*, November 9, 2012. http://www .dallasnews.com/business/top-100/headlines/20121109-container-store -leaps-to-top-spot-by-being-employee-centric.ece. 2011 sales: "2013: 100 Best Companies to Work For," *Fortune.com*, n.d. http://money.cnn.com /magazines/fortune/best-companies/2013/snapshots/16.html.

Chapter 7

1. Nudd, Tim. "Ad of the Day: Patagonia," *Adweek*, November 28, 2011. http://www.adweek.com/news/advertising-branding /ad-day-patagonia-136745.

2. Brady, Shirley. "Are You Buying Patagonia's 'Don't Buy this Jacket' Campaign?'" *Brandchannel*, November 30, 2011. http://www.brand -channel.com/home/post/2011/11/30/Patagonia-Dont-Buy-This -Jacket-113011.aspx.

3. Vickie Achee, Head of North American Marketing, Patagonia, personal interview with Denise Lee Yohn on January 13, 2012.

4. "November 28 Email: Don't Buy This Jacket," Patagonia website. http:// www.patagonia.com/email/11/112811.html.

5. Kroll, Luisa. "The Forbes 400: The Richest People in America," *Forbes*, September 19, 2012. http://www.forbes.com/sites/luisakroll/2012/09/19 /the-forbes-400-the-richest-people-in-america/. Pérez-Peña, Richard. "Facebook Founder to Donate $100 Million to Help Remake Newark's Schools," *New York Times*, September 22, 2012. http://www.nytimes .com/2010/09/23/education/23newark.html.

6. Brady, Diane. "Volunteerism as a Core Competency," *Bloomberg Businessweek*, November 8, 2012. http://www.businessweek.com /articles/2012-11-08/volunteerism-as-a-core-competency.

7. AT&T Aspire website homepage, AT&T website. http://www.att.com /gen/press-room?pid=2631.

8. Dawkins, Jenny, and Stewart Lewis. "CSR in Stakeholder Expectations: And Their Implication for Company Strategy," *Journal of Business Ethics*, May 2003. http://im.univie.ac.at/fileadmin/user_upload/proj_wind -sperger/KFK/KfK/CSR.pdf.

9. Edelman Research. "5 Years of Purpose: The Reengineering of Brand Marketing," Scribd.com, 2010. http://www.scribd.com/doc/90411623 /Executive-Summary-2012-Edelman-goodpurpose%C2%AE-Study.

10. Dawkins and Lewis, "CSR in Stakeholder Expectations."

11. Edelman Research, "5 Years of Purpose."

12. Gerzema, John, and David Roth. "Reputation, Purpose and Profits: Bridging the Gap," *Brandz Top 100 Most Valuable Global Brands 2012*, n.d., p. 11. http://media.rtl.nl/media/financien/rtlz/2012/2205brandsgeheel .pdf.

13. Ibid.

14. Ibid.

15. "Create Jobs for USA One Year Anniversary," Starbucks.com, November 2, 2012. http://news.starbucks.com/article_display.cfm?article_id=714.

16. Champniss, Guy. "Your Sustainability Message: Not Enough Charisma to Light Up the Room?" *CSR Newswire*, July 20, 2012. http://www.csrwire .com/blog/posts/473-your-sustainability-message-not-enough-charisma -to-light-up-the-room#.

17. Silverthorne, Sean. "The Vanguard Corporation," *HBS Working Knowledge*, October 5, 2009. http://hbswk.hbs.edu/item/6295.html.

18. Ibid.

19. Chouinard, Yvon. *Let My People Go Surfing* (London, England: Penguin Books), 2005.

20. "Our Reason for Being," Patagonia.com. http://www.patagonia.com/us /patagonia.go?assetid=2047&ln=140.

21. "Patagonia's Footprint Chronicles," Patagonia.com. http://www .patagonia.com/us/footprint/.

22. Smith, Daniel P. "The Help After the Storm," *QSR Magazine*, May 2011. http://www.qsrmagazine.com/exclusives/help-after-storm.

23. "Chipotle Backing Veggie U with Classroom Program," FastCasual
    .com, August 16, 2012. http://www.fastcasual.com/article/199065
    /Chipotle-backing-Veggie-U-with-classroom-program.

24. "Hear All About It: New Technology for Guests Who Are Hard of
    Hearing," ShakeShack.com, February 26, 2013. http://www.shakeshack
    .com/2013/02/26/hear-all-about-it-new-technology-for-guests-who
    -are-hard-of-hearing/.

25. Mohan, Anne Marie. "Is CSR Dead? Study Shows 'Brand Citizenship'
    More Important to Consumers," *Packaging World*, October 1, 2012.
    http://www.packworld.com/sustainability/corporate-social-responsibility
    /csr-dead-study-shows-brand-citizenship-more-important.

26. Don Fox, CEO, Firehouse Subs, personal interview with author Denise
    Lee Yohn on May 29, 2012.

27. Ibid.

28. Ibid.

29. "Hero Cup," FirehouseSubs.com, 2013. http://www.firehousesubs.com
    /Hero-Cups.aspx.

30. "Franchise Overview," FirehouseSubs.com, 2013. http://www.firehouse
    -subs.com/Franchise-Overview.aspx.

31. "How You Can Help," FirehouseSubs.com, 2013. http://www.firehouse
    -subs.com/How-You-Can-Help.aspx.

32. Fox, Don. "San Diego." Private e-mail message to author Denise Lee
    Yohn, January 19, 2013.

33. Don Fox, personal interview.

34. Ibid.

35. Ibid.

36. Cheng, Beiting, Ioannis Ioannou, and George Serafeim. "Corporate
    Social Responsibility and Access to Finance," *HBS Working Knowledge*,
    July 22, 2011. http://hbswk.hbs.edu/item/6766.html.

37. Ioannou, Ioannis, and George Serafeim. "The Impact of Corporate Social
    Responsibility on Investment Recommendations," Harvard Business
    School, August 2010. http://www.hbs.edu/faculty/Publication%20
    Files/11-017.pdf.

38. Bennett, Drake. "Social+Capital, the League of Extraordinarily Rich
    Gentlemen," *Bloomberg Businessweek*, July 26, 2012. http://www
    .businessweek.com/articles/2012-07-26/social-plus-capital-the-league-of
    -extraordinarily-rich-gentlemen.

39. Ibid.

40. Little, Amanda. "An Interview with Patagonia Founder Yvon Chouinard," Grist.com, October 23, 2004. http://grist.org/article/little-chouinard/.

41. Winter, Caroline. "Patagonia's Latest Product: A Venture Fund," *Bloomberg Businessweek*, May 6, 2013. http://www.businessweek.com /articles/2013-05-06/patagonias-latest-product-an-in-house-venture-fund.

42. "The First Ever Innocent Annual Report," Innocent Drinks, 2007. http:// www.innocentdrinks.co.uk/AGM/innocent_annual_report_2007.pdf.

43. Stockdale, Sue. "Innocent Drinks: Profile of Richard Reed, the Fruit Smoothie King," EvanCarmichal.com, n.d. http://www.evancarmichael .com/Women-Entrepreneurs/2910/Innocent-Drinks-profile-of-Richard -Reed-the-fruit-smoothie-king.html.

44. Ibid.

45. "GE Launches Program to Develop Environmental Technologies," GreenBiz.com, May 11, 2005. http://www.greenbiz.com/news/2005/05/11 /ge-launches-program-develop-environmental-technologies.

46. LaMonica, Martin. "Stirring GE's Ecomagination," CNET.com, October 26, 2007. http://news.cnet.com/stirring-ges-ecomagination /2008-11392_3-6215496.html.

47. "About the Challenge," Ecomagination.com, n.d. http://challenge .ecomagination.com/ct/a.bix?c=ideas.

48. "The Winning Partners," Ecomagination.com, n.d. http://challenge .ecomagination.com/ct/e.bix?c=ideas.

49. "Data Visualization: GE's Ecomagination Challenge One Year Later," Ecomagination.com, n.d. http://visualization.geblogs.com/visualization /ecochallenge/.

50. Stevenson, Seth. "Patagonia's Founder Is America's Most Unlikely Business Guru," *Wall Street Journal*, April 26, 2012. http://online.wsj.com /article/SB10001424052702303513404577352221465986612.html.

51. Ibid.

52. Caglar, Deniz, Marco Kesteloo, and Art Kleiner. "How Ikea Reassembled Its Growth Strategy," *Strategy+Business*, May 7, 2012. http://www.strategy -business.com/article/00111?pg=all.

53. Ibid.

54. Ibid.

55. Ibid.

56. Ibid.

57. Ibid.

58. Ibid.

59. "LYFE Kitchen Announces Final Menu from Chefs Art Smith and Tal Ronnen," LYFEKitchen.com, September 29, 2011. http://restaurants .lyfekitchen.com/wp-content/uploads/2013/05//5MenuRelease.pdf.

60. "LYFE Kitchen Delivers a Comfortable Haven Dedicated to Environmental Responsibility," LYFEKitchen.com, December 1, 2011. http://lyfekitchen.wordpress.com/2011/12/01/lyfe-kitchen-delivers-a -comfortable-haven-dedicated-to-environmental-responsibility/.

61. Kaufman, Frederick. "Former McDonald's Honchos Take On Sustainable Cuisine," *Wired*, July 31, 2012. http://www.wired.com/business/2012/07 /ff_lyfekitchens/all/.

62. Ibid.

63. "Social and Environmental Assessment Report," BenJerry.com, November 28, 2012. http://www.benjerry.com/cms/site/us/lang/en_US/home /company/sear-reports/sear-2011.

64. Ibid.

65. Muir, John. *My First Summer in the Sierra* (Boston: Houghton Mifflin, 1911). John Muir said, "When we try to pick out anything by itself, we find it hitched to everything else in the universe."

Chapter 8

1. "About Sharp," Sharp.com, n.d. http://www.sharp.com/about/index.cfm.

2. Huber, Adele J. *Effective Strategy Implementation: Conceptualizing Firms' Strategy Implementation Capabilities and Assessing Their Impact on Firm Performance* (Wiesbaden, Germany: Gabler, 2011).

Acknowledgments

I never fully appreciated what a blessing my network of friends and colleagues is until I embarked on the journey of writing this book. The generous support, help, and encouragement I've received have been truly overwhelming.

I'd like to thank my clients with whom I've had the honor to work. Out of respect for confidentiality, I've kept you unnamed—but you are some of the world's greatest brands and it's been a privilege to be a part of your brand-building efforts.

I'm particularly grateful to my amazing partners and colleagues, who have inspired and taught me so much: David Aaker, Jack Abbott, Tom Asacker, Marti Barletta, Vivienne Bechtold, Ilise Benun, Susan Bratton, Stephanie Burns, Reid Carr, Ken Coogan, Scott Davis, Cammie Dunaway, Dain Dunston, John Fishback, Mike Fox, Annette Franz-Gleinicki, Lisa Freedman, Chris Gaebler, John Gerzema, Terri Graham, Craig Hoffman, Sally Hogshead, Erich Joachimsthaler, Andrea Kates, Sondra Kiss, Kevin Kruse, John Lee, Scott Lininger, Tom Loker, Om Malik, Bryan Mattimore, Steve McKee, Les McKeown, John Moore, Mike Moran, Steve Morris, Jon Mueller, David Murphy,

Bryan O'Rourke, Michelle Panik, Shawn Parr, Joe Pine, Steve Portigal, Amon Rappaport, Mary-Ann Somers, Jim Stengel, Sandra Szlachtianchyn, Michael Tchong, Kip Tindell, Mark Tomaszewicz, Stephanie Weaver, and John Willig. I'm sure I've left people off this list who are important to me—please forgive the oversight.

The people who graciously allowed me to interview them for this book deserve a special thank you: Vickie Achee, Peter Fader, Don Fox, Randy Garutti, Laura Klauberg, and Sean O'Connor.

Thanks especially to the teams at Jossey-Bass, Cave Henricks Communications, Shelton Interactive, and Greenleaf Book Group.

And, thank you, Noel Weyrich, for helping me get this book out of my head and onto the page, and Genoveva Llosa, for believing in me and this book from the very beginning.

About the Author

Denise Lee Yohn is a brand-building consultant, speaker, and writer who has been inspiring and teaching companies how to operationalize their brands to grow their businesses for twenty-five years. A former vice president and general manager of brand and strategy for Sony, Denise now offers her brand-building expertise to world-class organizations including Frito-Lay, New Balance, Oakley, and Jack in the Box. Blending a fresh perspective and a talent for inspiring audiences, she has addressed national audiences at conferences including the Consumer Electronics Show, National Restaurant Show, and American Marketing Association, and has been featured in publications including the *Wall Street Journal*, the *New York Times*, *USA Today*, *BusinessWeek*, *Harvard Business Review*, and *Advertising Age*.

For more information or to get in touch with Denise, please visit www.deniseleeyohn.com.

Want to join the conversation about *What Great Brands Do*? Denise is creating a virtual collage of great brands in action and invites your submissions via social media. To participate, please take photos of great brands you see and tag them with the hashtag #WGBD on Twitter or Instagram. You can learn more about this campaign to showcase great brands in action at www .deniseleeyohn.com/wgbd.

Index